Assessing and Developing Communication and Thinking Skills in People with Autism and Communication Difficulties

of related interest

Promoting Social Interaction for Individuals with Communicative Impairments
Making Contact
Edited by M. Suzanne Zeedyk
ISBN 978 1 84310 539 8

Succeeding with Interventions for Asperger Syndrome Adolescents
A Guide to Communication and Socialisation in Interaction Therapy
John Harpur, Maria Lawlor and Michael Fitzgerald
ISBN 978 1 84310 322 6

Group Interventions for Children with Autism Spectrum Disorders
A Focus on Social Competency and Social Skills
Albert J. Cotugno
ISBN 978 1 84310 910 5

Making Sense of Children's Thinking and Behavior
A Step-by-Step Tool for Understanding Children with NLD, Asperger's, HFA, PDD-NOS,
and other Neurological Differences
Leslie Holzhauser-Peters and Leslie True
ISBN 978 1 84310 888 7

First Steps in Intervention with Your Child with Autism
Frameworks for Communication
Phil Christie, Elizabeth Newson, Wendy Prevezer and Susie Chandler
Illustrated by Pamela Venus
ISBN 978 1 84905 011 1

Communicating Partners
30 Years of Building Responsive Relationships with Late-Talking Children including Autism,
Asperger's Syndrome (ASD), Down Syndrome, and Typical Development
Developmental Guides for Professionals and Parents
James D. MacDonald
ISBN 978 1 84310 758 3

Communication Issues in Autism and Asperger Syndrome
Do we speak the same language?
Olga Bogdashina
ISBN 978 1 84310 267 0

Enabling Communication in Children with Autism
Carol Potter and Chris Whittaker
ISBN 978 1 85302 956 1

Assessing and Developing Communication and Thinking Skills in People with Autism and Communication Difficulties

A Toolkit for Parents and Professionals

Kate Silver, Autism Initiatives

Jessica Kingsley Publishers
London and Philadelphia

First published in 2005
by Jessica Kingsley Publishers
116 Pentonville Road
London N1 9JB, UK
and
400 Market Street, Suite 400
Philadelphia, PA 19106, USA

www.jkp.com

Copyright © Autism Initiatives 2005
Printed digitally since 2009

Library of Congress Cataloging in Publication Data
Silver, Kate.
   Assessing and developing communication and thinking skills in people with autism and communication diffi-
culties : a toolkit for parents and professionals / Kate Silver, Autism Initiatives.
      p. cm.
   ISBN-13: 978-1-84310-352-3 (pbk.)
   ISBN-10: 1-84310-352-4 (pbk.)
   1. Autistic children—Language. 2. Autistic children—Education. 3. Autistic children—Rehabilitation. 4.
Communicative disorders in children—Diagnosis. 5. Communicative disorders in children—Treatment. 6.
Thought and thinking—Study and teaching. 7. Communication—Study and teaching. I. Title.
   RJ506.A9S55 2005
   618.92'85882—dc22
                                                                                        2005005199

British Library Cataloguing in Publication Data
A CIP catalogue record for this book is available from the British Library

ISBN 978 1 84310 352 3

Contents

The Background to the Communication and Thinking Skills Assessments and Curricula

The communication assessment and curriculum

The communication assessment record (CAR) was devised to be used with learners with an autistic spectrum disorder (ASD). Typically their acquisition of communication skills does not follow a normal developmental pattern, but descriptive recording facilitates observation of progress and change as it occurs.

The CAR provides a descriptive summary of an individual's communication skills. It has been devised to record a description of how a learner is communicating, what he[1] uses his communication for, what level of language he understands and how he interacts in a social context. When the CAR is revisited, it is then possible to note progress and change in the development of communication skills; for example, over a period of time, a learner may not have changed the length of phrases he uses, but he may use his communication skills confidently in more situations or with more people. Accurate recording on this assessment shows this progress.

When working with people to develop their skills, it is important that we complete an assessment that:

- looks at the areas of functioning that we consider important to the learner's development and progress

- tells us the level that a learner is at. If we are to target our teaching at an appropriate, effective level, we need to know the level at which a learner is functioning.

---

[1] For ease, 'he' is used throughout the assessment to mean 'the learner'. Obviously the learner may be male or female.

We must record and measure learners' progress in order to evaluate our input and make relevant amendments to our approaches. A curriculum enables us to focus on prime needs. We may then focus on what we may expect to cover during our teaching. The communication curriculum (CC) provides a source from which we may select relevant targets.

The communication assessment record

The CAR was developed in a school for pupils with autism.

We were keen to carry out assessment of communication and related skills and to record progress, but we found it difficult to find an assessment procedure that looked at the areas that we considered most important when working with pupils with autism.

It is well recognised that people with autism may have some difficulty in acquiring verbal language skills, but, most importantly, that people with autism frequently have difficulty *using* their language skills to communicate effectively, regardless of the level of their language skills.

Difficulties in understanding spoken language are common. These may often relate to people's weaknesses in using other cues to support their comprehension of language and in considering more than one interpretation of something that they may have seen or heard. For example, when language is interpreted literally, it is because only a single meaning has been considered. In order to reach the relevant interpretation, it is necessary to consider the context and other interpretations of the words. So, in learners with autism, it seems that development of thinking skills is inextricably linked to development of comprehension of spoken language. It was therefore considered necessary to include assessment of thinking skills alongside assessment of communication.

First, we wanted to look at the communication skills that an individual has available to him and we wanted to look at how he *uses* those skills in everyday situations. We know that a feeling of success is important to all learners' skills development, so we were particularly interested in the recognition of situations where a learner communicates most successfully and the factors necessary to help him to communicate successfully.

Obviously assessment of comprehension of language is of paramount importance, but, rather than looking at comprehension of spoken language in isolation, we wanted to consider the visual cues that an individual may use to support his understanding. It is important for most people with autism to learn strategies early in life which they may use to support their long-term difficulties in understanding spoken language.

In order to grasp a full picture of how an individual is communicating, it is necessary also to consider attention focus and social interaction. Effective communication cannot take place in isolation from social interaction. Some ability to control attention focus is necessary to learn from people and situations and to develop communication skills.

We have found it helpful to look at the communication skills used by a learner at home as well as at school. Often, a learner may use communication skills in different ways in the two environments. We have found it useful to complete an 'assessment of communication at home record' in discussion with a family member, rather than to send the record home for completion. Staff may then discover what a family are finding most difficult in terms of their child's communication and initial targets may address these difficulties in order to support the family situation. Also, where a learner is using skills in one environment, but not in the other, school and home may work together to generalise use of a learned skill from one environment to another.

There are many assessments that look at comprehension and use of language, but we found that in a 'test' situation, a pupil with autism may well respond in a completely different way to the way he would respond in a familiar or routine environment. Pupils with autism frequently have marked difficulties in generalisation of skills and so we felt it important that an assessment recognised this and looked at a skill being used in several situations. Several 'scales' are in use in special schools, which measure a pupil's progress in certain areas. While these scales can be useful, we felt that the skills measured in these scales were frequently not specific to pupils with autism. So, for example, it could be possible for a pupil with marked echolalia, but very limited ability to *use* communication effectively, to score quite highly on the communication scale.

We felt that a descriptive record would provide us with more useful information than a record which relied on a score alone. A descriptive record not only describes a learner's level of functioning for assessment purposes, but the description is equally useful for all staff working with that individual, particularly cover or supply staff. The summary pages following each of the two parts of the CAR provide a useable 'pen picture' of an individual.

Because of the demand to 'quantify' progress, we added the quantification summary sheet (QSS). This gives some 'measure' of progress, where this is required.

The communication curriculum

The assessment process is always important, but it becomes more useful if it then informs teaching. We devised the CC to support staff's working knowledge of the development of communication and related skills. There are direct cross-references between the CAR and the CC. Numbers in the CAR refer to numbers in the CC. So, following assessment, staff may refer to the CC to determine which skills should be taught.

Staff find the CC useful when planning new Individual Education Plans (IEPs) and when planning teaching sessions. They are able to look at where a pupil is at on the curriculum and identify 'gaps' in skills that may then be worked on, or they may look sequentially, to plan which skill to work on next.

We believe that the general teaching curricula and everyday real-life situations are the vehicles for teaching identified communication, social skills and thinking skills targets. There are therefore no prescribed or recommended activities for individual communication curriculum targets. We have found that all social situations, such as breaktime and lunchtime, are of particular value. However, all sessions may be adapted to allow targets for communication and related skills to be included. Science, design and technology and literacy lessons are particularly useful.

The thinking skills assessment record and curriculum

We recognise that development of communication skills – in particular development of understanding of spoken language – and of thinking skills are inextricably linked. For example, inviting an individual to respond to presented choices is often considered one of the most effective ways of helping someone to use language. But, in order to make a choice, it is necessary first to shift attention focus from one alternative to the other, then to consider the consequences of each alternative in turn, then to compare the alternatives by thinking between the two outcomes and deciding which would be preferable. Such 'side to side' thinking, where one thing is considered then another, is very difficult for people with ASD who typically think in 'straight lines'. Only once all the necessary thinking has been carried out, can language or other communication be used to convey the choice made.

We use thinking skills to support our understanding of situations. We look around and piece together information in order to work out what may be going on (i.e. to grasp an overview). We then use thinking skills to work out the most likely or meaningful interpretation of what is happening. Our interpretation of the situation then supports our understanding of language relating to that situation. We must consider alternatives in order to understand implied meaning and avoid literal interpretation.

When people are unable to use thinking skills to think ahead and imagine what may be about to happen, they find it difficult to make sense of language relating to things that they cannot see and they may perceive unexpected events as 'shocks', which may cause them anxiety.

When selecting areas of thinking to be considered in the thinking skills assessment record (TSAR) and curriculum, we selected those areas which we considered to have the greatest impact on ability to understand spoken language and to make sense of situations, and which thus affect anxiety levels. The TSAR is not intended to be a comprehensive assessment of thinking skills, but rather a support for the communication assessment and curriculum. It is intended to be descriptive in the same way as the CAR.

The thinking skills curriculum (TSC) may be used to identify teaching targets in the same way as the CC.

How we use the communication assessment and curriculum and the thinking skills assessment and curriculum

The communication assessment and curriculum and the thinking skills assessment and curriculum were developed in a school for pupils with autism. They are used in the school by a speech and language therapist working with teaching staff. The speech and language therapist and the teaching staff work together to complete the assessment records. Targets are then selected from the curriculum by the speech and language therapist, in conjunction with the teaching staff. Where helpful, the speech and language therapist is able to further break down or 'personalise' targets from the curriculum. Teaching staff also use the curricula to assist them in development of general class teaching targets. The assessments and curricula have been particularly helpful when the school was without a speech and language therapist for a short period of time. Teaching staff were then able to use the assessments to determine a pupil's level of functioning and then the curricula to devise IEPs for pupils.

Note

The communication assessment and curriculum and the thinking skills assessment and curriculum have been compiled by a practitioner for practitioners. The contents are based on experientially-based evidence of what works.

The Communication Assessment Record

Introduction

Ideally, the communication assessment record (CAR) should be completed by somebody who knows the learner well and who sees the learner in different situations throughout the day. In order for the assessment to be most useful, it should be completed with as much relevant detail as possible and with examples of the way in which language is used or understood. Where a skill is not used at all by the learner, 'not applicable' may be recorded.

The assessment tool is divided into two parts, part I and part II. Usually only part I or part II of the assessment will be completed, depending on an individual's level of development of communication skills, but occasionally sections from both parts will be relevant and then all relevant sections may be completed. As a general rule, part I will be relevant to learners from those communicating without words through to those communicating using two or three words together. Part II is relevant to those who are using phrases of three and more words. There is a summary sheet at the end of each part. This may be completed in order to give an overview of the information in the assessment and is useful when a 'pen picture' of an individual's communication skills is required.

The CAR is a tool. It may be used in the following ways:

- When the CAR is completed, both strengths and weaknesses in all areas of communication are readily identified.

- The CAR is cross-referenced to the communication curriculum (CC). The codes are as follows:
  'E' – expressive communication, 'EU' – use of communication,
  'U' – understanding of communication, 'S' – social interaction,
  'TS' – thinking skills. This means that where an area of weakness is identified, a relevant target may be selected from the CC.

- The descriptive detail within the CAR means that an unfamiliar person may quickly learn how an individual communicates and how he is best motivated and helped to use and understand communication.

- When reassessment takes place, the descriptive format of the CAR enables changes in patterns of use of communication to be identified, and functional progress in use of communication to be recognised more readily than when communication is assessed solely by more traditional methods (e.g. number of words linked, grammatical accuracy).

The CAR may form part of the baseline assessment carried out in a school.

Note

We have included a glossary so that people using the CAR may be clear about what is meant by some of the words used in the assessment.

When the CAR has been completed, the quantification summary sheet (QSS) may be completed.

Communication Assessment Record I

In order to assess the current level and type of interaction/communication of the individual, complete this assessment record with as much relevant detail as possible, giving examples of the way in which language is used or understood by the learner.

The codes E1, EU3, U6 etc. in this assessment record refer to aspects of the communication curriculum. After the assessment, you can refer to the curriculum in order to identify skills targets to work towards.

Name: _____

Date: _____

Assessment completed by: _____

☐ Expressive Communication I

☐ Functional Use of Communication I

☐ Understanding of Communication I

☐ Social Interaction I

☐ Summary Sheet

Expressive Communication I

E1 E2 E3	1. Are words or vocalisations used?
E3 E4	2. Are gestures, signs or symbols used?
E8	3. Is there immediate or delayed echolalia? (i.e. does he repeat what has been said by someone else?) Please give examples.
E3 E4	4. If single words are used, please give examples of the most frequently used.
E3 E5	5. Does he name objects and/or pictures? Please give examples.
E6	6. Does he use any verbs?
E7 E8	7. Does he create phrases of his own? Please give examples.
EU18	8. Are the words clear?
EU19	9. If signs are used, are the signs clear?

Functional Use of Communication 1

EU2   1. How is 'no' or 'I don't want to' indicated?

EU3   2. How does he make requests?

E1
EU2   3. Do sounds or actions carry meaning e.g. hand biting, nipping?
EU3
EU13

E2   4. Is a first finger point used?

EU3   What for?

EU6   5. What most motivates him to communicate (e.g. food, Disney, computer)?

EU13   6. Is he able to give directions/instructions to other people? (e.g. 'sit down', 'there', 'Gill mix')

   To whom?

   Where?

✔

EU4
EU5

7. Is communication directed appropriately towards another person?

To whom?

In which contexts?

EU20   8. Does he initiate communication?

How? (e.g. words, signs, actions)

Does this vary with people and contexts?

EU6
EU8
EU9
EU10

9. Are words learned and used as part of the daily routine? (e.g. snack time)

EU7   10. Is he able to request help when faced with a problem?

EU8
EU10

11. Is there generalisation of words learned in daily routines to new situations? (e.g. snack time to other food times)

EU13
EU16
EU17

12. When upset/distressed, what does he do?

Can he indicate what the problem is, or indicate how he is feeling?

EU12   13. How does he gain attention?

EU19   14. Does he draw others' attention to things he finds interesting?

EU15   15. Does he question or seek information? How?

16. How can you help the individual to use his communication skills? (e.g. does he respond to prompts such as sentence completion or pointing?)

EU6
EU9
EU10

17. Where is he most communicative? (e.g. computer, lunch)

EU4
EU11

18. With whom does he communicate most?

19. Is language used relevantly and appropriately in context?

Understanding of Communication 1

U1   1.   Attention control – comment on his ability to attend to a task in groups and one-to-one situations.

U5   2.   Listening and memory skills – what is his level of auditory memory?
U6
U7
U15

U3   3.   Does he use gesture, signs, symbols or the written word as an aid to understanding spoken language?

         When?

         How?

U2   4.   Does he respond to his name, 'no' or 'stop'?
U4

         Does he follow situational directions, such as 'get your shoes'? Please give examples.

U5   5.   Can he understand nouns? (e.g. cup, biscuit, car)

U6   6.   Can he understand verbs? (e.g. running, jumping)

7. Can he understand the following words phrased in grammatically simple questions, within the 'here and now'?

U9   What?

U8
U9   Where?

U14   Who?

Please give examples of when/where he understands these questions.

U12   8. Can he understand simply phrased language relating to
the immediate past? (things that have just happened)

U13   the immediate future? (things that are about to happen)

Please give examples of when he has used language in this way.

U11   9. Can he understand language relating to just beyond the 'here and now?' (e.g. shift attention focus from an instruction relating to activity at the table, to an instruction to fetch object from cupboard)

U16   10. Can he understand language relating away from the 'here and now' to familiar or particularly salient events or places? (e.g. relating to outings or home)

11. Comment on speed of language processing (e.g. do you allow 'extra' time for him to process spoken language? How much?)

✔

Social Interaction I

S1   1. Is joint attention established?

2. At what level does he interact with others?

S3   Uses others as tools

S7   Uses others for people play

S9   Enjoys and seeks out company

S3   3. Does he take part in 'give and take' activities with others?
S4

S3   4. Comment on interaction with peers in
S4   structured time
S5

       non-structured time

S12   5. How does he respond when others initiate interaction with him?

6. Comment on eye contact in
structured time

non-structured time

S6
S13
7. Comment on turn-taking in
structured time

non-structured time

S8
8. Comment on desire/ability to take part in turn-taking games where staff copy him.

S10
9. Comment on desire/ability to copy actions, sounds or words.

S13
10. Comment on ability to share.

When?

How?

S11
S12
11. Comment on ability to respond to and give social greetings.

When?

How?

✓

Communication Assessment Record I:
Summary Sheet

Expressive Communication	Functional Use of Communication
Understanding of Communication	Social Interaction

Communication Assessment Record II

In order to assess the current level and type of interaction/communication of the individual, complete this assessment record with as much relavant detail as possible, giving examples of the way in which language is used or understood by the learner.

The codes E1, EU3, U6 etc. in this assessment record refer to aspects of the communication curriculum. After the assessment, you can refer to the curiculum in order to identify skills targets to work towards.

Name: _____

Date: _____

Assessment completed by: _____

☐ Expressive Communication II

☐ Functional Use of Communication II

☐ Understanding of Communication II

☐ Social Interaction II

☐ Summary Sheet

Expressive Use of Communication II

1. Are the words in sentences used in the right order? Are words missed out in sentences? Is there evidence of word finding difficulty?

E12   Comment on grammatical accuracy.

E13   Comment on vocabulary (naming objects and concepts)

E11   2. When he is telling you something (e.g. about an event at home or TV programme), does he retell the event in the right order or does he have difficulty sequencing what he wants to say, and waffle or ramble?

EU18   3. Are the speech sounds clear?

EU18   4. Is the speech fluent?

E8   5. Are most phrases used his own phrases or does he use immediate and/or delayed echolalia?

Functional Use of Communication II

1. Does he have favourite topics that he likes to talk about, and does he often turn the conversation towards these?

What are his favourite topics?

2. How do you encourage him to use his language?

EU33 3. Can he maintain a topic of conversation without introducing ideas that to you seem irrelevant to what you are talking about?

4. Does he use language to

EU28 ask questions? Please give examples of most frequently used phrases.

EU30 seek information?

problem solve?

Who does he ask?

Where?

EU31 5. Does he use language to say how he is feeling?

EU16 6. Does he use language to indicate when he has a problem?

In which contexts – relating to a problem in the 'here and now' or a problem away from the 'here and now'?

EU27 7. Does he use language to give social greetings?

To whom?

When?

EU37 8. Does he use language to let you know when he does not understand?

EU41 9. Does he use language to apologise?

With/without prompts?

Appropriately/inappropriately?

To whom?

Where?

EU23   10. Does he use his language to retell things that happened
EU24   in the immediate past?
EU38

beyond the immediate past?

salient events only?

EU25   11. Does he use his language to predict/anticipate things that are going to happen
     in the immediate future?

beyond the immediate future?

salient events only?

EU22   12. How does he indicate refusal?

Does this vary with people or contexts?

EU29   13. Does he use his language to negate, i.e. to say 'no', 'no it's not' etc.?

EU39   14. Does he give instructions/directions to carry out a familiar task?

With or without visual clues?

With or without prompts?

15. Does he give explanations?

EU26   With concrete cues?

EU36   Without contrete cues?

EU44   16. Does he resolve conflict?

With whom?

Where?

When?

EU45   17. Does he achieve compromise?

EU42   Does he reason and negotiate?

Please give examples of use of these skills.

EU43   18. Does he give opinions?

In which contexts?

EU40   19. Does he interrupt politely?

EU46   20. Does he joke?

Appropriately?

Inappropriately?

Does he create his own humour?

Does he retell jokes?

EU33   21. Does he maintain a topic of conversation?

Does this depend on the topic?

Does this depend on people/contexts?

EU20   22. How does he initiate social interaction/communication?

EU34   23. Does he change topics appropriately, or lose you in topic changes?

EU35   24. Does he have awareness of saliency when
retelling?

sorting relevant/irrelevant information?

presenting most important information first?

EU39   25. Does he use abstract language to
give directions?

give instructions (e.g. to make a cup of tea)?

recommend how he would/could complete an activity?

26. Is language used to self?

In which contexts?

Why?

27. Does he join in conversation in a group situation?

Understanding of Communication II

1. Comment on speed of language processing.

2. Comment on comprehension away from the 'here and now'.

U17　　3. Comment on understanding of language beyond the immediate past.

U18　　4. Does he understand language relating to particularly salient events?

U19　　5. Can he understand language beyond the immediate future?

U21
U22　　6. What is his level of auditory memory?

7. Can he grasp the overview (i.e. can he recognise what something is 'all about' and complete the sentence, 'it's all about…') relating to an activity?

relating to a short story book

relating to spoken language when he has been given some information, e.g. about a concert

U24   8. Can he understand 'why' questions?

with concrete/very obvious cues, e.g. why won't it fit? (when obviously too big or too small)

in increasingly abstract contexts, e.g. why is he crying?

U27   9. Comment on his development of a concept of time and time-related vocabulary.

U28   Can he understand 'when' questions? (e.g. when did you go shopping? when are you going swimming?)

U25   10. Can he understand 'how' questions? (e.g. how did you make that? how did he hurt his leg?)

U29   11. Comment on his awareness of ambiguity/literal interpretation.

U30   12. Can he understand implied meaning?

U31   13. Can he draw inferences from situations?

spoken language?

U32   14. Can he understand idioms?

15. Does he understand
    humour?

    slapstick?

U33   jokes relying on play on words?

E13   jokes relying on vocabulary/knowledge?

16. Awareness of saliency – is he able to
    discriminate between relevant and irrelevant information?

    draw the main points from an activity?

U34   draw the main points from spoken information?

U37   17. Does he understand fantasy/reality boundaries?

18. Is he aware of his own weaknesses in comprehension and does he employ compensating
    strategies, e.g. use of the written word, copying others, requesting clarification?

19. Is he able to assimilate information to gain meaning, i.e. piece together information to 'get the
    picture'? (e.g. recognise an object from a series of clues – 'it's yellow, it's a fruit', 'you peel it, you
    can mash it')

Social Interaction II

1. Is he more talkative in certain situations or with certain people?

S16 2. Can he recognise feelings of anger, sadness, fear and happiness in self?

S17 3. Can he guess how you or others are feeling?
S19

4. Can he keep appropriate distance
S21   in conversation?

S20   in social situations?

S22 5. Can he give and maintain appropriate eye contact?

Is this variable with different people and contexts?

U37 6. Does he have an awareness of fantasy/reality?

S28 7. Does he respond when you initiate conversation?
S29

S23   8. Does he initiate conversation?

       With whom?

       Where?

       In one-to-one situations?

       In small groups?

S24   9. Does he take turns appropriately or 'hog' the conversation?

       Does this vary with the conversation partner(s)?

S25   10. Does he monitor the listener's response?

       How?

       When?

S26   11. Does he clarify what he has said when you do not understand?

       Is this with or without prompting?

S27   12. Is he an 'active' listener? Describe what he does when you are talking.

S28
S29
S33
13. How does he maintain or develop conversation?

S30
14. How does he terminate interactions?

Does he do this appropriately?

Is this variable with people and context?

S31
15. Does he respond appropriately when others terminate the interaction?

S32
16. Describe body movements/posture/fidgeting etc. during conversation.

S34
S35
S36
17. Is he aware of what the listener knows/doesn't know?

S39
18. Does the way he speaks vary depending on whom he is speaking to?

S18
19. Is appropriate stress, tone, volume and intonation used?

S37
20. Is he aware that it is possible to influence how others think and feel?

In what situations?

With whom?

S38
21. Does he know what to keep private?

Communication Assessment Record II: Summary Sheet

Expressive Communication	Functional Use of Communication

Understanding of Communication	Social Interaction

How we use the quantification summary sheet for the communication assessment record

The CAR may be used to record progress in development of communication skills.

By noting whether a certain skill becomes more consistently or less consistently used by a learner, progress may be measured. For example, 'following two word level instructions' may be recorded as 'sometimes' and when reviewed after a period of time may be recorded as 'frequently' thus reflecting progress. Or 'immediate echolalia' may be recorded as 'frequently' and later as 'rarely', also reflecting progress.

When learners are particularly anxious, their communication skills may differ from those skills used when they are relaxed and enjoying their usual patterns of communication. Skills developed initially such as physical communication or immediate echolalia may remain part of an individual's communication repertoire as further skills are developed, but these early skills may only be used when the individual is very anxious. This could be noted in the final column of the quantification summary sheet (QSS).

The Autism Initiatives CAR is intentionally a descriptive assessment record, aimed at creating an accurate picture of how a learner communicates and what motivates him to communicate. The QSS aims to quantify the description within the CAR. Clearly, there is variation in an individual's use of communication skills in different situations and with different people. These differences are recorded in the descriptive CAR and the QSS must take a more 'overall' or 'on average' view of a learner's communication skills.

The terms used within the QSS to record frequency of use of an individual skill are subjective. The aim is to develop the learner's communication skills in everyday environments. Artificial teaching and artificial 'testing' of use of a communication skill is seen as unhelpful. Testing the use of a communication skill in a 'test' situation only tests the use of the skill in the 'test' situation and does not necessarily reflect everyday use of the skill.

The terms used are:

- **N/A** – This means that a skill is not applicable to a learner. For example, 'accurate syntax' is not applicable to a learner using only single words to communicate.

- **Never** – This means that a learner never uses that skill.

- **Rarely** – This means that a learner has been observed using that skill, but on isolated occasions and probably not on a daily basis. When opportunity is given, the skill is probably used between 0 and 25 per cent of the time.

- **Sometimes** – This means that a learner uses that skill once or twice a day on average. When opportunity is given, the skill is probably used between 25 and 50 per cent of the time.

- **Frequently** – This means that the learner uses that skill several times a day. When opportunity is given, the skill is probably used between 50 and 75 per cent of the time.

- **Consistently** – This means that a learner almost always uses that skill where it would be relevant to do so, probably approaching 100 per cent of the time. There will be still exceptional times when the skill is not used, usually because of the learner's emotional state.

Core communication functions

At Autism Initiatives, we have identified certain communication functions which we believe to be 'core communication functions'. These are communication skills which we feel are essential life skills. It is our aim that each learner, whenever possible, should acquire these skills. As these skills are particularly important, they have been marked with an asterisk on the QSS.

Quantification Summary Sheet for the Communication Assessment Record

* An asterisk denotes a particularly important skill.

Name: ───────────────────────────────────

Date: ───────────────────────────────────

Expressive Communication

Frequency of use

	N/A	Never	Rarely	Sometimes	Frequently	Consistently	Notes about use of skill
1. Physical/non-verbal communication	☐	☐	☐	☐	☐	☐	
2. Signs/symbols/photos	☐	☐	☐	☐	☐	☐	
3. Immediate echolalia	☐	☐	☐	☐	☐	☐	
4. Delayed echolalia	☐	☐	☐	☐	☐	☐	
5. Nouns	☐	☐	☐	☐	☐	☐	
6. Verbs	☐	☐	☐	☐	☐	☐	
7. Two word links	☐	☐	☐	☐	☐	☐	
8. Creating own phrases (three or more words)	☐	☐	☐	☐	☐	☐	
9. Appropriate word order	☐	☐	☐	☐	☐	☐	
10. Accurate syntax	☐	☐	☐	☐	☐	☐	

Functional Use of Communication

Frequency of use

	N/A	Never	Rarely	Sometimes	Frequently	Consistently	Notes about use of skill
1. Refuses appropriately*	☐	☐	☐	☐	☐	☐	
2. Initiation of communication	☐	☐	☐	☐	☐	☐	
3. Use of first finger point	☐	☐	☐	☐	☐	☐	
4. Appropriate direction of communication	☐	☐	☐	☐	☐	☐	
5. Makes requests*	☐	☐	☐	☐	☐	☐	
6. Gives directions	☐	☐	☐	☐	☐	☐	
7. Words used within learned contexts/routines	☐	☐	☐	☐	☐	☐	
8. Requests help*	☐	☐	☐	☐	☐	☐	
9. Asks questions	☐	☐	☐	☐	☐	☐	
10. Able to indicate has problem*	☐	☐	☐	☐	☐	☐	
11. Communicaties without prompts	☐	☐	☐	☐	☐	☐	
12. Able to communicate in many contexts	☐	☐	☐	☐	☐	☐	
13. Communicates with variety of people	☐	☐	☐	☐	☐	☐	
14. Able to 'recall'	☐	☐	☐	☐	☐	☐	
15. Able to 'predict'	☐	☐	☐	☐	☐	☐	
16. Maintains topic of conversation	☐	☐	☐	☐	☐	☐	
17. Changes conversation topic appropriately	☐	☐	☐	☐	☐	☐	
18. Gives appropriate social greetings	☐	☐	☐	☐	☐	☐	
19. Indicates when he does not understand	☐	☐	☐	☐	☐	☐	
20. Apologises appropriately	☐	☐	☐	☐	☐	☐	
21. Able to give explanations	☐	☐	☐	☐	☐	☐	
22. Able to negotiate	☐	☐	☐	☐	☐	☐	

Understanding of Communication

Frequency of use

	N/A	Never	Rarely	Sometimes	Frequently	Consistently	Notes about use of skill
1. Attends to speaker*	☐	☐	☐	☐	☐	☐	
2. Situational understanding	☐	☐	☐	☐	☐	☐	
3. Uses visual cues as aid to understanding*	☐	☐	☐	☐	☐	☐	
4. Understands single nouns	☐	☐	☐	☐	☐	☐	
5. Understands single verbs	☐	☐	☐	☐	☐	☐	
6. Follows two word level instructions	☐	☐	☐	☐	☐	☐	
7. Understands 'what' and 'where' questions	☐	☐	☐	☐	☐	☐	
8. Understands 'who' questions	☐	☐	☐	☐	☐	☐	
9. Understands language relating to past	☐	☐	☐	☐	☐	☐	
10. Understands language relating to future	☐	☐	☐	☐	☐	☐	
11. Follows three word level instructions	☐	☐	☐	☐	☐	☐	
12. Understands 'why' questions	☐	☐	☐	☐	☐	☐	
13. Understands 'when' questions	☐	☐	☐	☐	☐	☐	
14. Understands ambiguous language	☐	☐	☐	☐	☐	☐	
15. Grasps implied meaning	☐	☐	☐	☐	☐	☐	
16. Grasps 'main point'	☐	☐	☐	☐	☐	☐	
17. Aware of fantasy/reality boundaries	☐	☐	☐	☐	☐	☐	
18. Able to assimilate information to 'get the picture'	☐	☐	☐	☐	☐	☐	
19. Employs strategies to support verbal comprehension (copies others, uses thinking skills to work out what to do, etc.)*	☐	☐	☐	☐	☐	☐	

Social Interaction

Frequency of use

	N/A	Never	Rarely	Sometimes	Frequently	Consistently	Notes about use of skill
1. Joint attention is established*	☐	☐	☐	☐	☐	☐	
2. Uses adults as tools	☐	☐	☐	☐	☐	☐	
3. Uses adults for people play	☐	☐	☐	☐	☐	☐	
4. Enjoys and seeks out adult company	☐	☐	☐	☐	☐	☐	
5. Able to 'give and take' objects with peers and adults*	☐	☐	☐	☐	☐	☐	
6. Able to 'take turns' with peers	☐	☐	☐	☐	☐	☐	
7. Copies actions/words with meaning in play situations*	☐	☐	☐	☐	☐	☐	
8. Uses eye contact appropriately	☐	☐	☐	☐	☐	☐	
9. Mutuality is established (enjoys sharing a wavelength with an adult)	☐	☐	☐	☐	☐	☐	
10. Aware of own emotional state	☐	☐	☐	☐	☐	☐	
11. Aware of emotional state of others	☐	☐	☐	☐	☐	☐	
12. Maintains appropriate social distance	☐	☐	☐	☐	☐	☐	
13. Takes appropriate conversational turns	☐	☐	☐	☐	☐	☐	
14. Monitors listener during conversation	☐	☐	☐	☐	☐	☐	
15. Gives clarification without prompting	☐	☐	☐	☐	☐	☐	
16. Terminates interactions appropriately	☐	☐	☐	☐	☐	☐	
17. Aware of listeners' knowledge	☐	☐	☐	☐	☐	☐	
18. Uses appropriate tone, volume and intonation	☐	☐	☐	☐	☐	☐	
19. Aware that can influence how others think or feel	☐	☐	☐	☐	☐	☐	
20. Aware of what to keep private	☐	☐	☐	☐	☐	☐	

The Communication Curriculum

Introduction

The communication curriculum (CC) was devised to help staff working with individuals with ASDs to select communication skills for development, when setting IEPs and when planning lessons.

The CC is presented in two parts. These correspond with parts I and II of the communication assessment record (CAR). At any one time an individual may be working within part I or part II, but, depending on individual patterns of acquisition of communication skills, may have targets drawn from both parts I and II.

Each part of the CC includes:

- expressive communication (the communication skills/language that the pupil has available to use)

- functional use of communication (what the individual uses his communication skills for)

- understanding of communication

- social interaction.

In order to maximize development of each learner's communication skills, all activities in the classroom should encourage development of skills in each of these four areas in all learners. Individual aims may target an area(s) considered most important to each individual's development of communication skills at that time. Each learner may therefore have aims taken from two, three or four of these areas at any one time.

When working on expressive language with learners with ASD, we consider that generally, targets relating to use of language are more important than targets relating to the grammatical content of language. We have found that work on grammatical aspects of language is usually most effective when inability to use a certain aspect of grammar is making it difficult for the child to be understood – for example, when confusion with tense forms is leading to confusion for the listener. Both staff and pupil are thus motivated to increase grammatical accuracy.

It is not intended that the CC should 'prescribe' an order of acquisition of communication skills. Rather, it provides a general guide or structure. We acknowledge that within a 'band' (series of targets) of the CC, learners will acquire skills in different orders and at different rates. The curriculum sequence therefore provides only an approximate guide to order of acquisition.

Some ordering of the targets within the CC reflects experience of working with learners with ASDs, rather than normal developmental patterns. For example, we teach 'ask for help' early in communication development, as experience has shown that this is a useful skill for pupils with ASDs to learn. It leads to reduction of frustration and challenging behaviour and effectively teaches the pupil that communication with other people can be useful.

When selecting targets from the CC, it is essential to consider individual autistic learning patterns, needs and motivation to communicate. This means that targets will not always be taken from the CC in a sequential order. The CC may however be useful to highlight 'gaps' in skills and will be useful as part of the process of identification of future targets.

Development of communication skills is central to all other aspects of learning. Development of communication must therefore link closely with other areas of learning. Many of the targets within the CC link directly with targets relevant to other curricula, particularly literacy and science. When writing IEPs, it is therefore possible to link work on communication directly with work on other curriculum areas.

Communication Curriculum I

Expressive Communication I

E1   To actively indicate needs and wants without recognisable words, e.g. using vocalisation or behaviour patterns

E2   To develop a vocabulary of personally motivating single words

E3   To develop a first finger point
To develop a vocabulary of personally motivating single symbols
To develop a vocabulary of personally motivating single signs
One, two or all above methods of communication to be used according to individual preference

E4   To use 'effect' words, e.g. more, no, stop, gone, me/mine/my turn, ready steady go, open

E5   To use single nouns

E6   To use single verbs

E7   To link words/symbols to create two and more word phrases

E8   To add to learned/echolalic phrases to create own phrases

---

Notes

Functional Use of Communication I

EU1	To respond to forced alternatives/choices, using symbols, signs or words
EU2	To indicate refusal through single word, sign, gesture or vocalisation
EU3	To use communication to indicate needs and wants
EU4	To communicate with familiar adult, e.g. key worker
EU5	To direct communication towards another person
EU6	To use single words in familiar everyday routine situations, e.g. snack time, lunchtime, setting up computer
EU7	To use communication to request help
EU8	To use learned phrases appropriately in relevant contexts
EU9	To use language in familiar contexts spontaneously without prompting
EU10	To use language in a variety of routine and novel situations
EU11	To communicate with less familiar adults and peers
EU12	To use communication to gain adult attention
EU13	To use communication to give directions/instructions
EU14	To use 'there' to respond to 'where?' questions
EU15	To question
EU16	To use communication to indicate a 'problem'
EU17	To communicate feelings of anger appropriately
EU18	To use systems to support spoken language where the spoken word is not clear, e.g. symbols, written word
EU19	To comment to adult on something interesting
EU20	To initiate social interaction appropriately

Notes

Understanding of Communication I

U1   To attend to an activity with adult support

U2   To understand context dependent language through interpretation of situational cues, e.g. 'It's lunchtime', 'Get your coat'

U3   To use photos and objects as aids to understanding spoken language

U4   To understand 'no' and 'stop'

U5   To understand single nouns in concrete contexts, e.g. 'Give me the jam' (while extending hand to remove the need to understand 'give me')

U6   To understand single common verbs, e.g. sit down, sleep, run

U7   To understand two key words in concrete contexts, e.g. 'Give me the *scissors* and the *pen*'

U8   To understand 'where' questions in concrete contexts where the desired response is visible, e.g. 'Where's Joshua?', 'There'

U9   To discriminate between 'what' and 'where' questions within concrete contexts, e.g. 'What's that?', 'Where's the...?'

U10   To follow language immediately beyond the 'here' where a shift in attention focus is required, e.g. during table top activity follow request to get milk from the fridge, during table top activity looking at clothes follow language relating to own clothes.

U11   When cued in through linguistic and visual cues, to follow language relating to just beyond the immediate environment, e.g. when in the classroom, follow language relating to familiar places – 'Go to music', 'Go to the kitchen'

U12   To follow language supported by visual cues to refer to the immediate past, e.g. talk about an activity while things used in the activity are still out, or talk about a book as soon as it is finished

U13   To follow language relating to the immediate future – what we are going to do next
      • with strong visual cues, e.g. object
      • with weakening visual cues, e.g. photos, symbols

U14   To understand 'who' questions within concrete contexts

U15   To follow phrases containing three key words in concrete contexts, e.g. 'Give me the..., the... and the...' or 'Go to the cupboard and get... and...'

U16   When cued in through linguistic and visual cues, to follow language relating to a very familiar context away from the here and now, e.g. during activity about animals, to follow language referring to animals at home

Notes

Use of visual cues, objects, symbols and written word to be encouraged at all levels to support understanding of spoken language

Social Interaction 1

S1   To share attention focus with an adult, i.e. to focus jointly on an activity with an adult

S2   To receive objects from a familiar adult during activities

S3   To pass objects to familiar adults and peers

S4   To receive objects from peers

S5   To carry out activities alongside peers

S6   To take turns in structured activities with adults and peers with adult support

S7   To participate in interaction games, e.g. row the boat, chase, rough and tumble

S8   To take part in turn taking copying games with adult, where adult copies the child, e.g. banging a drum, blowing raspberries

S9   To initiate personally motivating game by approaching adult, e.g. rough and tumble, sheet games, copying games

S10   To imitate adult actions during turn taking and copying games

S11   To initiate social greeting at own level, e.g. to touch adult, give eye contact, say 'hello'

S12   To respond appropriately at own linguistic level to social greeting by adult, e.g. give eye contact, touch adult, use 'hello'

S13   To take turns in small group situations with minimal adult support

S14   To imitate actions and activities of peers in group situations, e.g. recognise that everybody else is standing up so stand up, wave when everybody else is waving

---

Notes

52

Communication Curriculum II

Expressive Communication II

E9 To use more than one phrase during a single conversational turn. (Phrases may not be grammatically linked, e.g. 'Went to shop, Mum and Dad. Got video. Video "Aristocats".')

E10 To develop creativity in language use, by creating own novel phrases of three and more words, i.e. reduced use of delayed echolalia

E11 To sequence phrases correctly when giving information

E12 To increase grammatical complexity and grammatical accuracy of language used, including:
- using pronouns appropriately
- marking past tense appropriately
- using 'because' appropriately
- marking future tense
- using appropriate question forms
- marking plurals

E13 To increase vocabulary to include:
- vocabulary relating to emotion
- vocabulary relating to time
- vocabulary relating to abstract concepts e.g. same and different comparatives

---

Notes

Functional Use of Communication II

FU21   To use communication confidently to talk about a variety of topics in a variety of situations

FU22   To refuse appropriately, e.g. 'No…', 'Don't like…'

FU23   To recall activities or events just beyond the immediate past, e.g. to talk about morning events at lunchtime

FU24   To recall salient activities removed in time and space, e.g. to recall particularly interesting weekend/evening/holiday/classroom activities

FU25   To predict future events, e.g. talk about what you are going to do,
- relating to just beyond the immediate future, e.g. to the afternoon activities
- relating to particularly salient future activities, e.g. a trip, a holiday

FU26   To give simple explanations relating to concrete events in the here and now, e.g. 'It won't fit! Why?', 'Because it's too big'

FU27   To give appropriate social greetings

FU28   To ask 'wh–' questions to seek information and to solve problems, e.g. 'Where's…?', 'Who's got…?'

FU29   To negate, i.e. to use 'No', 'No it's not!', 'It's not there!', etc.

FU30   To use other question forms to seek information and to solve problems, e.g. 'Do you want…?', 'Do you like…?'

FU31   To communicate own feelings of anger, sadness, fear and happiness.
cf. E13 Development of vocabulary

FU32   To give increasingly complex explanations within the 'here and now' with visual cues, e.g. respond to 'Why can't we…?', 'What would happen if…?', 'What do we need?', 'Why do we need it?'

FU33   To maintain a topic of conversation

FU34   To make topic switches relevant and clear to the listener

FU35   To show awareness of saliency when retelling
- to include relevant and exclude irrelevant information
- to order information giving the most important information/main point first

FU36   To give increasingly abstract explanations relating away from the 'here and now', e.g. respond to 'How did you…?', 'How do you know?', 'Why did you…?'

FU37   To indicate non-comprehension of spoken language

FU38   To recall information that does not directly relate to self, that is not own experience, e.g. during an activity, a student discovers that someone dislikes lemons, and recalls this later

FU39   To give increasingly abstract instructions/directions, e.g. to give directions to make a drink/a sandwich etc. before the 'making' is started

FU40   To interrupt politely

FU41   To apologise appropriately

FU42   To use language to reason and to negotiate

FU43   To give opinions

FU44   To use communication and thinking skills to resolve conflict

FU45   To use communication and thinking skills to achieve compromise

FU46   To joke appropriately where a sense of humour is developed

Notes

Understanding of Communication II

U17 To understand language relating to events beyond the immediate past, e.g. language relating to morning events at lunchtime

U18 To understand language relating to *particularly salient* past and future events, e.g. enjoyed trips out, weekend events

U19 To understand language relating to beyond the immediate future, e.g. to afternoon events at lunchtime

U20 To understand language relating to familiar people and places outside the 'here and now', e.g. to follow language relating to home, to family, to swimming pool, etc. when in school

U21 To develop auditory memory at three word level and above

U22 To deliver messages containing two to three word level phrases, i.e. to retain information over time and space

U23 To grasp an overview of spoken information, i.e. recognise we're talking all about…

U24 To understand increasingly abstract 'why' questions

U25 To understand 'how' questions

U26 To increase comprehension of syntax: to recognise tense markers/plurals/pronouns

U27 To develop a concept of time and understanding of relevant time vocabulary, e.g. before, after, morning, afternoon

U28 To understand 'when' questions within own concept of time

U29 To understand ambiguity and be aware of literal interpretation

U30 To understand implied meaning

U31 To draw inferences

U32 To understand everyday idioms, e.g. raining cats and dogs, catch red-handed

U33 To understand jokes relying on a play on words

U34 To draw the main points from spoken information

U35 To be aware of own weaknesses in comprehension and employ compensating strategies, e.g. use of written word, request for clarification of information given etc.

U36 To understand metaphor, e.g. he is a raging bull

U37 To be clear about fantasy/reality boundaries

Notes

Social Interaction II

S15 To demonstrate awareness of others in small group situations, i.e. to take turns appropriately, know whose turn it is, recall information about group members ('Who had the tambourine? Who had the shaker?')

S16 To recognise feelings of anger, sadness, fear and happiness in self

S17 To interpret facial expression, body posture and movement and gesture in others

S18 To use appropriate voice volume and tone

S19 To interpret change in voice volume and tone in others

S20 To understand social rules regarding social physical contact

S21 To maintain appropriate social distance

S22 To maintain appropriate eye contact

S23 To initiate conversation appropriately

S24 To take turns during conversation

S25 To monitor listener response and recognise listener boredom and confusion

S26 To be helpful to the listener – to clarify or curtail language used

S27 To be an active listener – to maintain eye contact, offer acknowledgement, e.g. 'hmm', 'yes'

S28 To maintain and develop a conversation in a one-to-one situation

S29 To maintain and develop conversation in small group situations
(skills developed in EU31, 32, 35, 38 will be necessary)

S30 To terminate conversation or interaction appropriately

S31 To interpret social cues and respond appropriately to others' termination of interaction

S32 To maintain control of body movements during interaction, i.e. to develop awareness of fidgeting, head movements, etc.

S33 To maintain appropriate response times during conversation

S34 To demonstrate empathy with familiar adults and peers

S35 To be aware of what others know and don't know

S36 To adapt information given according to listeners' knowledge

S37 Comprehension of cause, effect and consequences in social interaction

S38 To be aware of what to keep private

S39 To adapt communicative style to social situation, e.g. adopt more formal style for unknown person or person in authority

---

Notes

The Thinking Skills Assessment Record

Introduction

We recognise the importance of developing the thinking skills of people with ASDs. Experience has shown that high anxiety levels often result from an individual's difficulty in working out what may be happening in a given situation or coping with a situation which is not turning out as originally expected. Such anxiety is often due to rigid patterns of thought. We have therefore found it helpful to begin to assess and address the development of flexible thinking skills with our learners.

The thinking skills assessment record (TSAR) provides a descriptive summary of an individual's thinking skills. It is not comprehensive, but assesses certain areas of thought. Development of skills in each of these areas increases the ability to piece together information to derive meaning and to consider alternatives. Thinking in this way promotes the development of flexible thinking and reduces dependence on 'straight line' or rigid thinking. Development of the ability to think ahead and to problem solve is essential for effective planning and organizsing.

As with the CAR, it is best if the TSAR is completed by people who know the individual well and see the individual in many daily situations. The information recorded in the assessment will be derived from observation of the individual. Sometimes staff may wish to set up informal situations where they may assess ability in certain areas. Where staff are uncertain about what to record in certain areas, they may use the thinking skills curriculum (TSC) to help them to know what skills to look for and record.

Upon completion, the TSAR will provide a detailed description of a pupil's thinking skills at the time of completion.

Note that individuals working within part I of the CC, would not be expected to have understanding of ambiguity, implied meaning or truth value, so these sections should be recorded as 'not applicable'.

The TSAR is a tool and it may be used in the following ways:

- It is possible to identify 'gaps' where there are weaknesses in skills. These gaps may then be targeted using the TSC. Relevant aims may then be incorporated into IEPs.

- Because the assessment is descriptive, progress may be noted when reassessment takes place. It is possible to note whether there has been any change in a pupil's ability to think within each area or whether skills have been acquired in a 'new' area.

Core thinking skills

Attention focus: To shift attention focus from speaker to activity or activity to speaker.

Choices: To make appropriate choice from two visible items. To consider alternatives when making choice (in all situations).

Sequencing and planning: To predict within daily activities using visual clues where necessary.

Deduction and inference: To work out what is going to happen by looking at a group of objects within a familiar situation.

Problem solving: To recognise a 'problem' within daily situations. To employ a problem solving strategy (such as asking for 'help', seeking necessary object to solve problem, etc.).

Categories: To sort objects that 'go together' such as toothbrush and toothpaste, swimwear and towel, etc.

Awareness of thoughts and feelings (social cognition): E.g. to be aware of self feeling 'cross'.

Note

The ability to *consider alternatives* is important and should be prioritised.

Thinking Skills Assessment Record

In order to assess the current level and type of thinking skills of the individual, complete this assessment record with as much relevant detail as possible, giving examples of the way in which thinking skills are used. Please provide descriptive comments on the individual's abilities in the following areas. The thinking skills curriculum may be used as a guide to aid note writing if necessary.

The codes TAF, TC, TP etc. in this assessment record refer to the section in the thinking skills curriculum where develeopment of these skills is addressed. After assessment, you can refer to the curriculum in order to identify skills targets to work towards.

Name: _____

Date: _____

Assessment completed by: _____

✓

TAF   1. Attention focus

TC   2. Ability to make choices

TP   3. Ability to predict

TD   4. Ability to deduct meaning from things and situations

TPS   5. Ability to solve problems

TCa   6. Awareness of categories

TSD   7. Awareness of similarities, differences and comparisons

TSC   8. Awareness of own thoughts and feelings

TO   9. Ability to grasp overview and main points

TA   10. Awareness of ambiguity

TI   11. Awareness of implied meaning

TTV   12. Ability to consider truth value (whether something is true/makes sense)

TT   13. Awareness of own skills as a thinker

How we use the quantification summary sheet for the thinking skills assessment record

The TSAR may be used to record progress in development of thinking skills. In addition to the description within the TSAR, the quantification summary sheet (QSS) may be used.

We have identified core thinking skills. These are skills which we believe to be most important in the development of functional flexible thinking skills. These are the thinking skills that are included in the QSS.

By noting whether a certain thinking skill becomes more, or less consistently used by a learner, progress may be measured.

The terms used within the thinking skills QSS to record frequency of use of an individual skill are the same as those within the communication assessment QSS and are subjective.

We aim to develop the learner's thinking skills in everyday environments. We avoid artificial teaching and artificial 'testing' of use of a thinking skill. Testing the use of a thinking skill in a 'test' situation only tests the use of this skill in that particular situation and would not necessarily reflect everyday use of the skill.

The terms are:

- **N/A** – This means that a skill is not applicable to a pupil. For example, somebody working within part I of the CC would not be expected to seek more than one interpretation of language or situations.

- **Never** – This means that a pupil never uses that skill.

- **Rarely** – This means that a pupil has been observed using that skill, but on isolated occasions and probably not on a daily basis. When opportunity is given, the skill is probably used between 0 and 25 per cent of the time.

- **Sometimes** – This means that a pupil uses that skill once or twice a day on average. When opportunity is given, the skill is probably used between 25 and 50 per cent of the time.

- **Frequently** – This means that the pupil uses that skill several times a day. When opportunity is given, the skill is probably used between 50 and 75 per cent of the time.

- **Consistently** – This means that an individual almost always uses that skill where it would be relevant to do so, probably approaching 100 per cent of the time. There will be still exceptional times when the skill is not used, usually because of the individual's emotional state.

Quantification Summary Sheet for the Thinking Skills Assessment Record

Name: _____

Date: _____

Thinking skill

Frequency of use

	N/A	Never	Rarely	Sometimes	Frequently	Consistently	Notes about use of skill
1. Shifts attention focus from activity to speaker	☐	☐	☐	☐	☐	☐	
2. Makes appropriate choice between two visible items	☐	☐	☐	☐	☐	☐	
3. Predicts within daily activities, using visual cues where necessary	☐	☐	☐	☐	☐	☐	
4. Works out what is going to happen by looking at objects within familiar situations	☐	☐	☐	☐	☐	☐	
5. Recognises a 'problem' within daily situations	☐	☐	☐	☐	☐	☐	
6. Uses a problem solving strategy	☐	☐	☐	☐	☐	☐	
7. Sorts objects that 'go together' e.g. swimwear and towel	☐	☐	☐	☐	☐	☐	
8. Aware of self feeling 'cross'	☐	☐	☐	☐	☐	☐	
9. Grasps overview of a situation/book/video/activity	☐	☐	☐	☐	☐	☐	
10. Aware of more than one interpretation of language or situations	☐	☐	☐	☐	☐	☐	
11. Aware of own ability to use thinking skills	☐	☐	☐	☐	☐	☐	

The Thinking Skills Curriculum

Introduction

People with an autistic spectrum disorder typically have rigid patterns of thinking. This means that they think in 'straight lines' and find it difficult to assimilate and integrate information. This in turn means that they find it difficult to access stored information in order to solve everyday problems or to support other skills.

We recognise that effective flexible thinking skills underpin success in development of effective communication and interaction skills. Effective flexible thinking skills contribute significantly to the development of self-esteem and reduce dependence on prompts from adults.

Thinking skills should be taught as an integrated part of the daily curriculum. Individuals should be encouraged to match and map new information onto their own existing knowledge or experience and to learn to store and access information effectively. The aim is to develop each individual's awareness of his ability to think and to solve problems.

The thinking skills curriculum (TSC) highlights the skills which individuals need to learn. It provides a framework, but is not intended to be prescriptive. It is not a 'programme'. It supports the maximising of the thinking skills of each individual.

The TSC highlights development in the following areas:

- attention focus

- choices

- sequencing and planning

- deduction and inference

- problem solving

- categories

- similarities and differences

- awareness of thoughts and feelings (social cognition)

- overview/main point of information

- ambiguity

- implied meaning

- truth value

- awareness of own skills as a thinker

Within each of the above areas there is a hierarchical progression. There is also some hierarchical progression through the different areas. For example, attention focus is essential for progress in all areas of learning, and awareness of implied meaning or truth value cannot be learned until other areas of flexible thinking are established. However, the development of thinking skills requires an integrated approach. This means that at any one time, an individual may have thinking skills objectives as part of his learning goals, working on one or more of the above sections.

'Core' thinking skills have been identified. These are listed at the start of the thinking skills assessment record (TSAR) and asterisked within the TSC. Teaching of these skills should obviously be prioritised.

It should be noted that the skill of *considering alternatives* is particularly important. Considering alternatives has not been designated a specific area of development, but is a skill to be developed in many of the areas identified for learning.

Links with other curricula

Development of thinking skills is inextricably linked with the communication curriculum (CC). Many linguistic skills require an ability to think effectively. There is therefore some overlap with the CC.

The TSC also has close links with the science curriculum in schools. Many of the skills necessary for science require thinking skills.

Thinking Skills Curriculum

* An asterisk denotes a core thinking skill.

Attention focus

TAF1	To focus on an activity
TAF2	To focus on a speaker
TAF3*	To shift attention focus from an activity to a speaker to an activity
TAF4	To attend to the 'broad' picture (as though using a wide angle lens), e.g. the room, the people
TAF5	To attend to detail within an activity (as though using a zoom lens), e.g. the picture on the table, the detail on the picture
TAF6	To shift attention focus between broad and detail focus, i.e. to look at the same thing in a different way

Notes

Choices

TC1*	To make appropriate choice from two visible items
TC2	To make appropriate choice from several visible items
TC3	To make appropriate choice from unseen objects using symbols or photos as prompts
TC4	To make choices between unseen objects using minimal prompts, e.g. where to go, what to do, what to use
TC5	To explicitly consider alternatives when making choice
TC6	To make choice from unseen but familiar items
TC7	To give reason for choice

Notes

Predicting, sequencing and planning

What will happen next...? (Consider alternatives/find information)

TP1   To predict within familiar routine, e.g. dressing

TP2*   To predict within daily activities where relevant objects are visible

TP3   To predict beyond the immediate future using knowledge of routine, situational cues

TP4   To predict using previous experience and knowledge, thinking skills, ability to recall and situational cues

TP5   To use flexible thinking to imagine what comes next in novel situations, i.e. to use all available cues to work out what is happening/going to happen

TP6   To plan course of action, considering alternatives

Notes

Deduction and inference

That means...

TD1*   To imagine what you are going to do by looking at a group of objects within a familiar situation, e.g. bread and toaster = make toast; ingredients and scales = bake a cake

TD2   To use symbols, photos and written word to work out what to do

TD3   To imagine what a book may be about by looking at the cover

Notes

Problem solving

'Problem' refers to any situation where things are not running smoothly. Note that all problem solving initially must be within the 'here and now'.

TPS1*   To recognise the problem within familiar situations, e.g. spilled drink, no fork, broken pencil, initially with prompting such as 'Oh dear' or 'What's the matter?' or 'What's the problem?'

TPS2   To solve the problem in response to a prompt, e.g. 'What do you need?'

TPS3   To solve the problem of 'What do we need?' within familiar activities such as baking, cutting and sticking or painting when some objects are missing but others are present and serve as visual cues

TPS4*   To solve familiar problems, e.g. spilled liquid, broken pen

TPS5   To recognise and label novel problems, i.e. recognise and label a problem which has not happened before, e.g. to respond to 'What's happened?' or 'What's the problem?'

TPS6   To employ strategies to solve novel problems, i.e. having identified what the problem is, begin to solve it. Prompts given initially to include 'What shall we do now?'. Problem solving strategies to be learned include:

- asking for help
- looking at what others are doing and doing the same if that appears to be working
- recalling previous experience and relating to current problem, e.g. recalling involvement in previous similar or identical experience and using that experience to solve current problem (initial prompts may include 'What did we do last time?')
- asking questions to gain information in order to solve the problem, e.g. 'Where's...?', 'Who's got...?', etc.
- using language to direct or control the problem, e.g. 'Stop...'
- thinking up solutions and alternatives, e.g. 'What can we use instead?', 'Where can we go instead?', 'How can we get there?'

Notes

Categories

TCa1   To sort two familiar objects into two piles or categories, e.g. swimming trunks, towels, knives, forks.

TCa2   To put like with like when sorting several objects, e.g. when tidying up put scissors with scissors, pens with pens, glue with glue, etc.

TCa3*   To identify things that 'go together', e.g. bowl and spoon, sponge and shower gel

TCa4   To sort objects into familiar categories with minimal prompting

TCa5   To use appropriate category labels, i.e. to respond to 'These are all...' clothes, food, etc.

TCa6   To identify the 'odd one out' or the different one within a group of familiar objects or pictures

TCa7   To imagine (think up) other unseen objects that could belong within a visible category, e.g. think of another animal, another vehicle

TCa8   To create own links between objects:

- to create own categories when sorting a group of objects
- to use appropriate category labels
- to identify things that go together with minimal prompting (with real objects and pictures such as 'things that go together' cards)
- to explain why objects go together, demonstrating awareness of own thinking
- to re-sort categories, i.e. to sort the same group of objects in different ways

Notes

Similarities and differences

TSD1   To select two objects which are the same from a group of objects

TSD2   To understand and use the word 'same'

TSD3   To indicate when two objects are not the same

TSD4   To understand and use the word 'different'

TSD5   To recognise attributes (e.g. size, colour, people's likes and dislikes) which are
- the same
- different

TSD6   To compare objects which are
- the same
- different
- similar

and to use these words when relating objects

TSD7   To explain the sameness, differences and similarities between items demonstrating awareness of own thinking

TSD8   To relate current experience to previous same experience (using phrases such as 'This is the same as…')

TSD9   To relate current experience to previous similar experience (using phrases such as 'It's like…', 'It reminds me of…)

Notes

Awareness of thoughts and feelings (social cognition)

TSC1*   To be aware of self feeling sad, angry and happy

TSC2   To be aware of the causes of these feelings

TSC3   To recognise when familiar people are sad, angry and happy

TSC4   To be aware of self feeling frightened, bored, annoyed, irritated

TSC5   To recognise feelings of anger, boredom etc. in others

TSC6   To imagine what may be the cause of these feelings in self and others

TSC7   To adapt own behaviour appropriately in order to:
- manage own feeling
- react appropriately to feeling in others

Notes

Overview/main point of information

TO1   To grasp an overview of an activity, i.e. to respond to 'It's all about...'

TO2   To grasp an overview of spoken language, books, i.e. to respond to 'It's all about...'

TO3   To sort relevant and irrelevant information in order to grasp the main points in
- pictures
- simple texts and books
- spoken language

TO4   To determine the purpose an activity

Notes

Ambiguity

TA1   To recognise that a picture may be interpreted in two ways
- shapes as individual shapes or as a house, etc.
- semantic interpretation, e.g. a man may be lying down, sleeping, or lying down, fallen over

TA2   To recognise that one word can have two meanings, e.g. glass

TA3   To recognise that one meaning can have two words, e.g. sofa, settee

TA4   To recognise everyday idioms, e.g. full of beans, hit the roof, etc.

TA5   To be aware that the same words can have different meanings when spoken in different contexts or in different ways, i.e. to be aware of pragmatics

TA6   To be aware of, and to attempt to discriminate between, lying, jokes, sarcasm, opinion and fact

Notes

Implied meaning

TI1   To derive meaning which is implicit rather than explicitly stated from
- situations
- written language, e.g. in books
- spoken language

Notes

Truth value

TTV1   To check information received both orally and written against own knowledge and experience. To consider 'Does this make sense?'

Notes

Awareness of own skills as a thinker

TT1   To respond to 'How do you know?' questions

TT2   To respond to 'why' questions

TT3   To develop awareness that what seemed impossible is now possible through thinking and problem solving

TT4   To be aware of 'what I know and what I don't know'

TT5   To be aware of 'what I need to know' in a given situation

TT6   To be aware of how to find out 'what I don't know' and 'what I need to know'

TT7   To evaluate own thinking

Notes

Glossary

The words below are used in the CAR, CC, TSAR and TSC but may not be familiar to all people working with pupils with ASDs. We have therefore included brief definitions of the words to help in completing the assessment and understanding the curriculum targets.

Active listener: a listener who looks and acts as though they are listening by e.g. looking, nodding, asking questions.

Ambiguity: where there are two interpretations or meanings, e.g. phrases such as 'pull your socks up', words such as glasses (to put on your eyes or to drink out of) or situations such as somebody lying on the floor, who may be sleeping or may be injured or unconscious.

Auditory memory: memory for spoken information. For example, some people have very short auditory memories, and can retain perhaps only a single word or single piece of spoken information.

Compensating strategies: strategies that may be used to help the pupil, e.g. writing things down, asking people to repeat what they have said, looking at what other people are doing.

Concrete cues: objects or people in the situation that give a clue to what is being talked about.

Conversational turn: one person's turn at talking during a two or more way conversation.

Delayed echolalia: where language learned as a chunk in one context is used in another context, e.g. in response to 'Where shall I put it?', the delayed echolalia response could be 'Put it in the bin' (a phrase learned as a whole). The delayed echolalia may or may not be relevant to the context.

Fantasy/reality: fantasy is anything that does not really exist or is not real.

Grammatical accuracy: using grammar accurately, for example, putting words in the correct order, appropriate use of pronouns, accurate verb tenses.

Idiom: a group of words whose meaning cannot be worked out from the words themselves, e.g. 'It's raining cats and dogs'.

Immediate echolalia: where language spoken to the pupil is repeated back immediately, e.g. in response to 'Do you want a drink?', the immediate echolalia response could be 'Want a drink' or 'drink'.

Immediate past: something that has just happened, e.g. the activity that has just been completed, playtime when the class has just come in.

Implied meaning: meaning that must be worked out from the context, e.g. 'It's cold in here' meaning 'Shut the window'.

In context: in a situation, so for example, a pupil will learn words in the context of snack time and use the words appropriately in this situation, but will not use those words in other situations or contexts.

Joint attention: where the pupil and somebody else both focus together on the same thing, sharing the attention focus.

Literal interpretation: interpreting or understanding the word at 'face value' without seeking the real meaning, e.g. 'I'm keeping my eyes on you' interpreted literally suggests that the person is going to take out their eyes and keep them on the person being spoken to.

Salient events: events that are particularly significant to the individual pupil.

Semantic classes: words belonging to the same category, e.g. animals, fruit.

Semantic relationships: words that are associated through meaning, e.g. things that go together, such as toothbrush and toothpaste, sandwiches and lunchbox.

Situational understanding: where language is understood only because of other clues in the situation. For example, 'Get your shoes' said by the door, with a coat on or 'Put it in the bin', handing over some rubbish that clearly belongs in the bin.

Word-finding difficulty: the feeling of knowing a word, but not being able to bring it to mind – that tip of the tongue feeling.

Visual cues: objects and people that are visible and give a clue as to what is being talked about.

Further Reading

Attwood, T. (1998) *Asperger's Syndrome: A Guide for Parents and Professionals.* London: Jessica Kingsley Publishers.

Cumine, V., Leach, J. and Stevenson, G. (1997) *Asperger Syndrome: A Practical Guide for Teachers (Resource Materials for Teachers).* London: Taylor & Francis Group.

Howlin, P. (1997) *Autism: Preparing for Adulthood.* London: Routledge.

Jordan, R. and Powell, S. (1995) *Understanding and Teaching Children with Autism.* London: John Wiley & Sons.

Kelly, A. (2001) *Talkabout: A Social Communication Skills Package.* Oxford: Speechmark Publishing Limited.

Spence, S. (1983) *Developments in Social Skills Training.* New York: Academic Press.

Español

Primer grado RECORTABLE

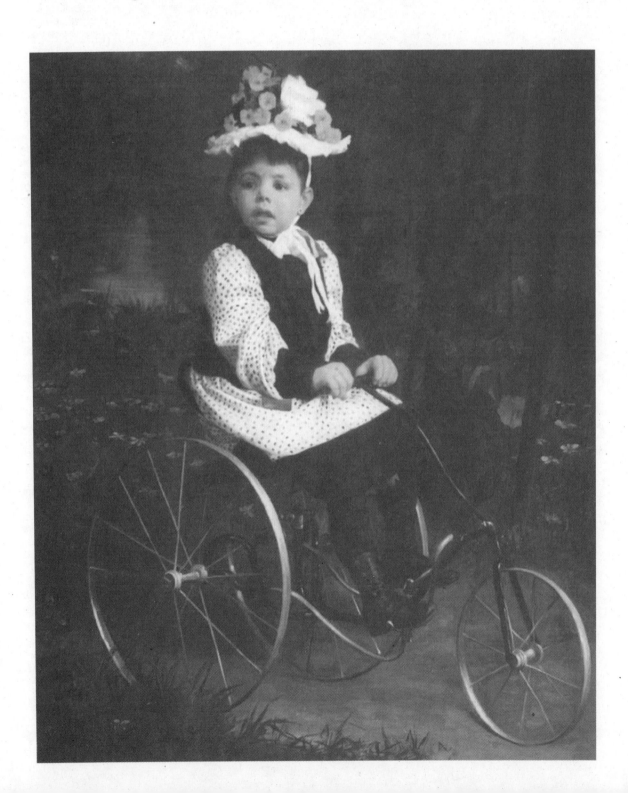

Español. Primer grado. Recortable fue elaborado por el Programa Nacional para el Fortalecimiento de la Lectura y la Escritura en la Educación Básica, con la colaboración de la Dirección General de Materiales y Métodos Educativos, ambos de la Subsecretaría de Educación Básica y Normal de la Secretaría de Educación Pública

Dirección del proyecto
Margarita Gómez Palacio

Recopilación y diseño de actividades
Laura V. González Guerrero,
Elia del Carmen Morales García (coordinadoras);
Ana Rosa Díaz Aguilar, Gregorio Hernández Zamora,
María Esther Salgado Hernández

Revisión
Lucía Jazmín Odabachian Bermúdez
Beatriz Rodríguez Sánchez
Fernando Bernal Acevedo

Colaboración
Zoila Balmes Zúñiga
Jorge Aníbal Coss Valdés
Laura Silvia Iñigo Dehud

Coordinación editorial
Elena Ortiz Hernán Pupareli
María Beatriz Villarreal González

Cuidado de la edición
José Manuel Mateo Calderón

Portada
Diseño: Comisión Nacional de Libros de Texto Gratuitos
Ilustración: *Niña en triciclo,* 1898
Óleo sobre tela, 136 x 96 cm
Germán Gedovius (1867-1937)
Casa de la Cultura de San Luis Potosí
Reproducción autorizada: Casa de la Cultura de San Luis Potosí
Fotografía: Rafael Morales Bocardo

Servicios editoriales
CIDCLI
Coordinación editorial e iconográfica:
Patricia van Rhijn y Rocío Miranda

Diseño:
Rogelio Rangel
  Annie Hasselkus
  Antonio Sierra
  Evangelina Rangel
Ilustración:
Gloria Calderas   Ana Ochoa
Juan Ezcurdia   Guadalupe Pacheco
Laura Fernández   Maribel Suárez
Luis Guerrero   Gerardo Suzan
Claudia Legnazzi   Tané, arte y diseño S.A.
Leonid Nepomniachi   Fabricio Vanden Broeck

Reproducción fotográfica:
Rafael Miranda

Primera edición, 1997
Tercera edición, 2001
Tercera reimpresión, 2004 (ciclo escolar 2005-2006)

D.R. © Secretaría de Educación Pública, 1997
     Argentina 28, Centro,
     06020, México, D.F.

ISBN 970-18-6814-5 (Obra general)
     970-18-6817-X

Impreso en México
DISTRIBUCIÓN GRATUITA-PROHIBIDA SU VENTA

Haz dos sobres para las letras móviles.

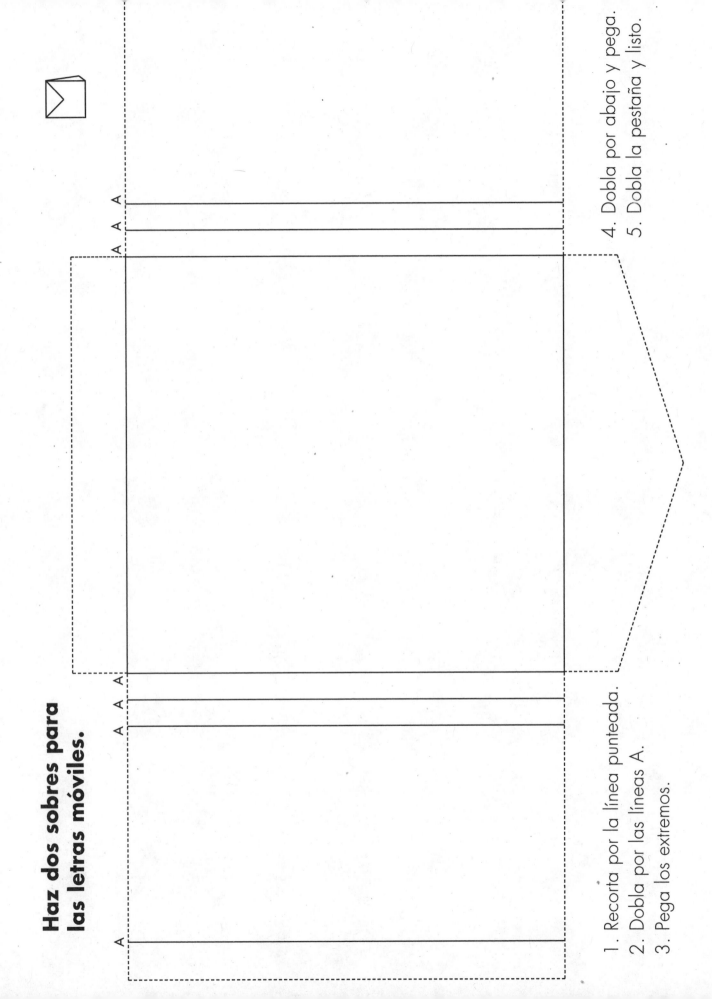

1. Recorta por la línea punteada.
2. Dobla por las líneas A.
3. Pega los extremos.
4. Dobla por abajo y pega.
5. Dobla la pestaña y listo.

a	a	a	b	b	b	c
c	d	d	d	e	e	e	f
f	f	g	g	g	h	h	h
i	i	i	j	j	j	k	k
k	l	l	l	m	m	m	n
n	n	ñ	ñ	ñ	o	o	o
p	p	p	q	q	q	r	r
r	s	s	s	t	t	t	u
u	u	v	v	v	w	w	x

x	x	y	y	y	z	z	z
a	a	a	a	e	e	e	e
i	i	i	o	o	o	u	u
u	t	t	t	p	p	p	l
l	l	m	m	m	s	s	s
r	r	r	n	n	n	f	f
f	f	y	y	j	j	j	j
X	X	Y	Y	Y	Z	Z	Z

A	A	A	B	B	B	C	C
C	D	D	D	E	E	E	F
F	F	G	G	G	H	H	H
I	I	I	J	J	J	K	K
K	L	L	L	M	M	M	N
N	N	Ñ	Ñ	Ñ	O	O	O
P	P	P	Q	Q	Q	R	R
R	S	S	S	T	T	T	U
U	U	V	V	V	V	W	W	X

Tiempo de escribir

 cama

 escuela

 jardín

 calle

 agua

 río

Reflexión sobre la lengua

 dormido

 cansado

 feliz

 herido

 enfermo

niño	papá	bosque
niña	mamá	árbol
pino	casa	jardín

Memorama de juguetes 1

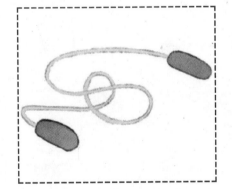

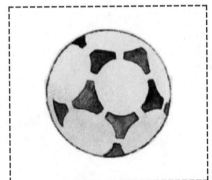

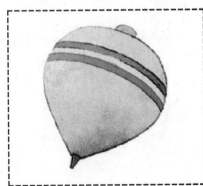

Memorama de juguetes 2

canicas	cubos	pelota
globos	balón	osito
muñeca	cuerda	yoyo
trompo	patines	balero

 Leer y compartir

perico

caballo

paloma

cochino

caracol

pato

cabrita

pez

pollo

conejo

perro

camello

 Hablar y escuchar

enojado

aburrido

contento

triste

asustada

Memorama de animales 1

Memorama de animales 2

pato	perro	león
lobo	toro	gato
rana	pollo	cabra
araña	oso	tigre

Colección de mariposas

Leer y compartir

Una cucaracha en la estufa.	La cucaracha mira los dulces.
La cucaracha se enfermó.	Y con un helado terminó.

Reflexión sobre la lengua

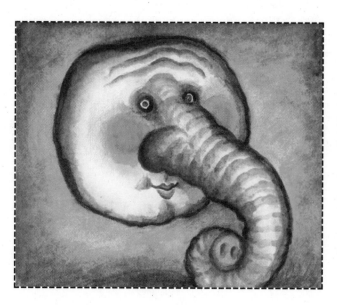

Memorama de animales y crías 1

Memorama de animales y crías 2

cabrita	gatito	cochinito
osito	conejito	perrito
changuito	patito	pececito

**Changuita
con falda**

**Changuita
con sombrero**

**Changuita
con traje de baño**

**Changuita
con vestido**

**Changuita
con tacones**

**Changuita
con rebozo**

Nombres de ropa

Hablar y escuchar

Nombres de animales

Tiempo de escribir

escondidas

yoyo

futbol

roña

cuerda

Leer y compartir

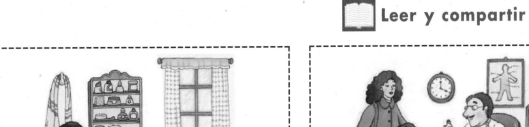

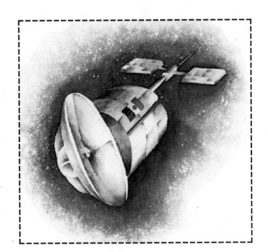

Lotería del espacio

Sol

estrellita fugaz.

Júpiter

Marte

Luna

Saturno

Lotería del espacio

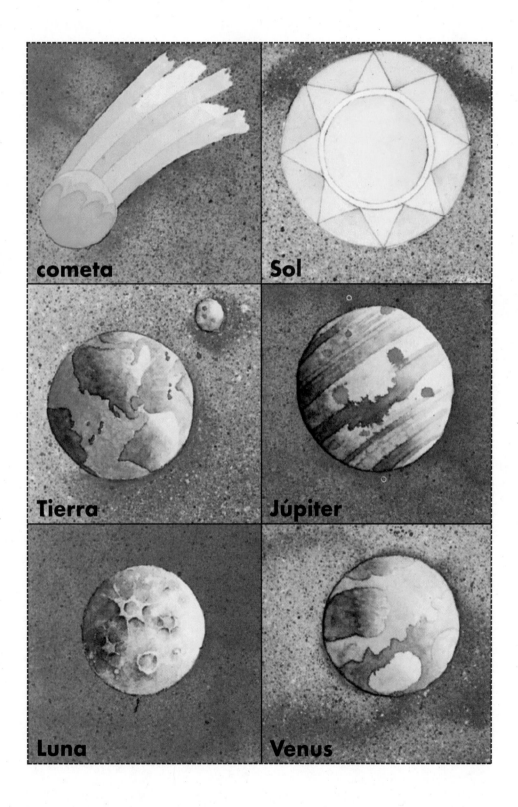

cometa

Sol

Tierra

Júpiter

Luna

Venus

Cartas del espacio

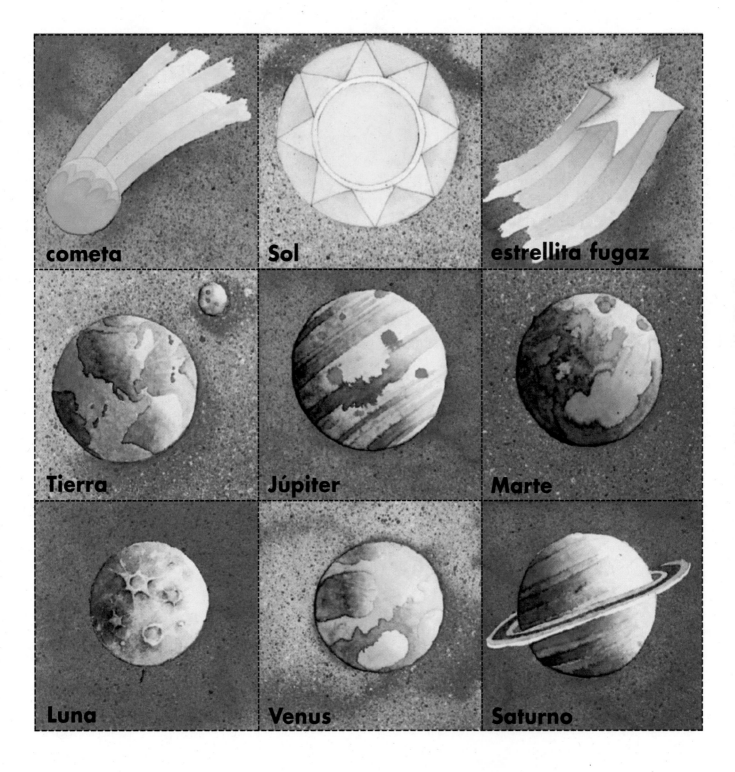

cometa

Sol

estrellita fugaz

Tierra

Júpiter

Marte

Luna

Venus

Saturno

 Leer y compartir

Planetas

 Plutón

 Urano

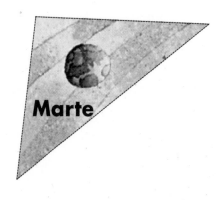 Marte

 Júpiter

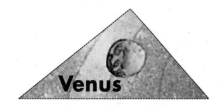 Venus

 Mercurio

 Neptuno

 Saturno

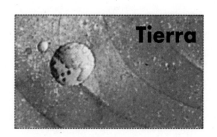 Tierra

Leer y compartir

Tiempo de escribir

el campo

la playa

la ciudad

mi mamá

mi hermano

mi maestra

tren

autobús

barco

Memorama de transportes 1

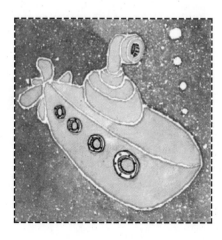  

Memorama de transportes 2

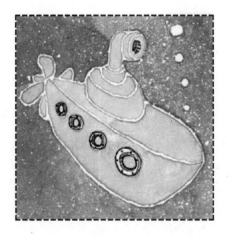  

barco	helicóptero	avión
tren	coche	autobús
lancha	bicicleta	submarino

📖 Leer y compartir

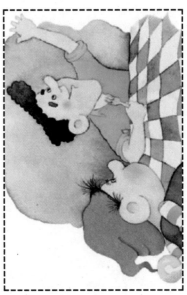

📖 Leer y compartir

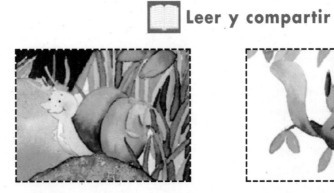

iguana

perro

gato

conejo

pájaro

pescado

Reflexión sobre la lengua

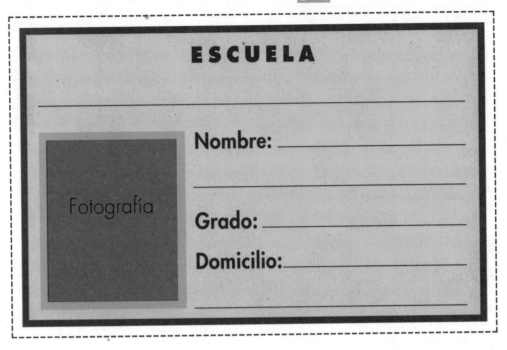

ESCUELA

Nombre: _____

Grado: _____

Domicilio: _____

Fotografía

13 • El gato bombero

Tiempo de escribir

pajarito

culebra

gato

pececito

iguana

conejo

ratita

tortuga

rana

perro

Hablar y escuchar

**Máscara
de papá
oso**

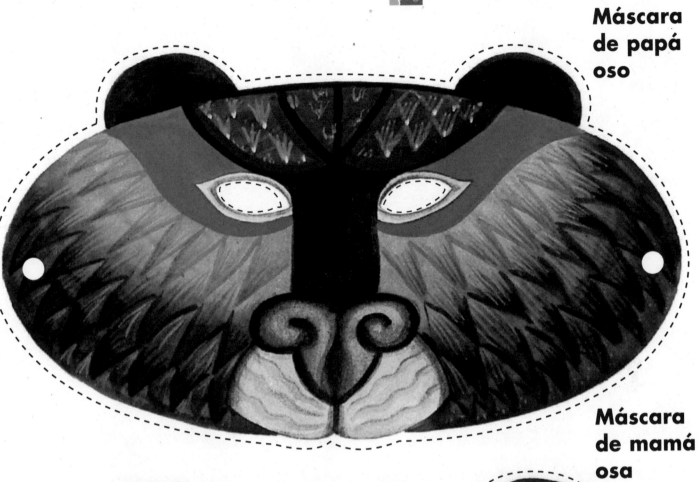

**Máscara
de mamá
osa**

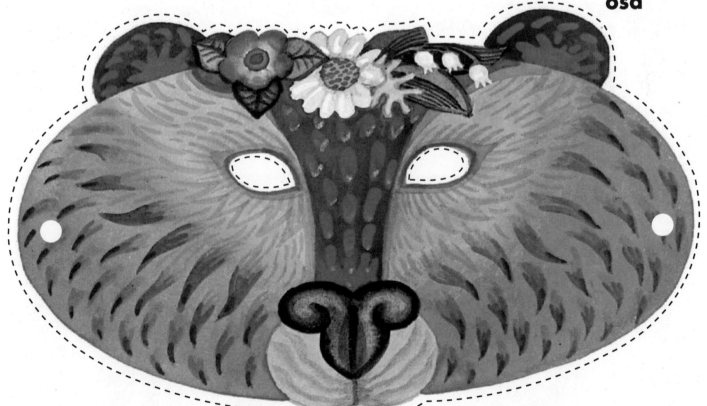

 Hablar y escuchar

**Máscara
de osito**

**Máscara
de Ricitos de Oro**

Leer y compartir

Hablar y escuchar

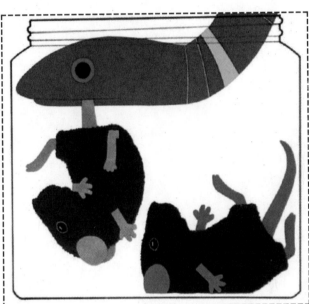

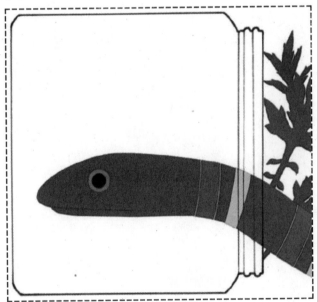

murciélago

serpiente

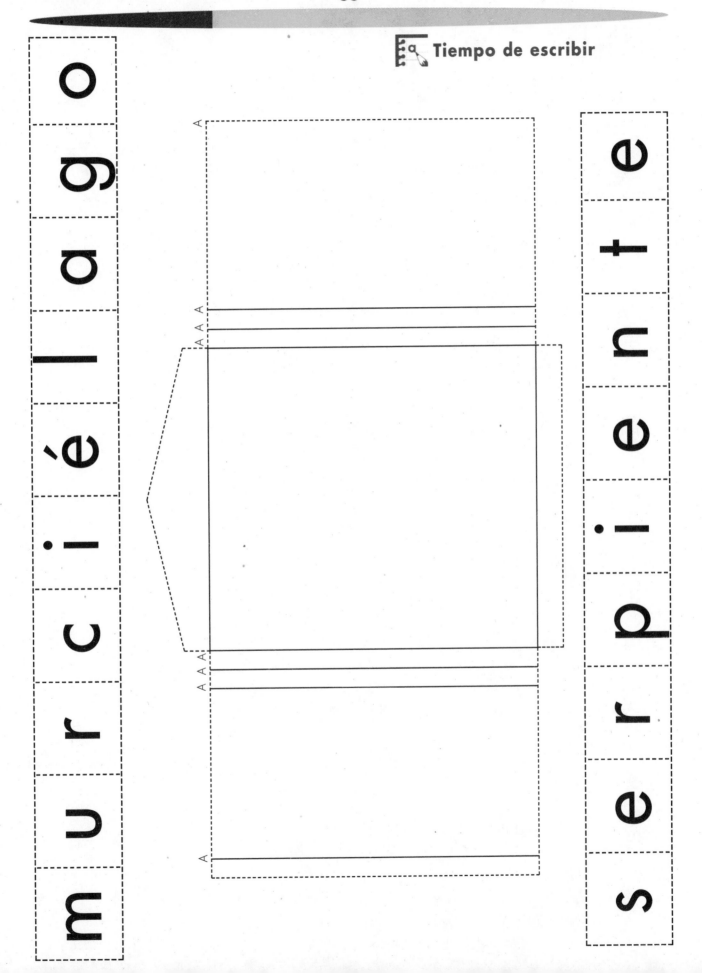

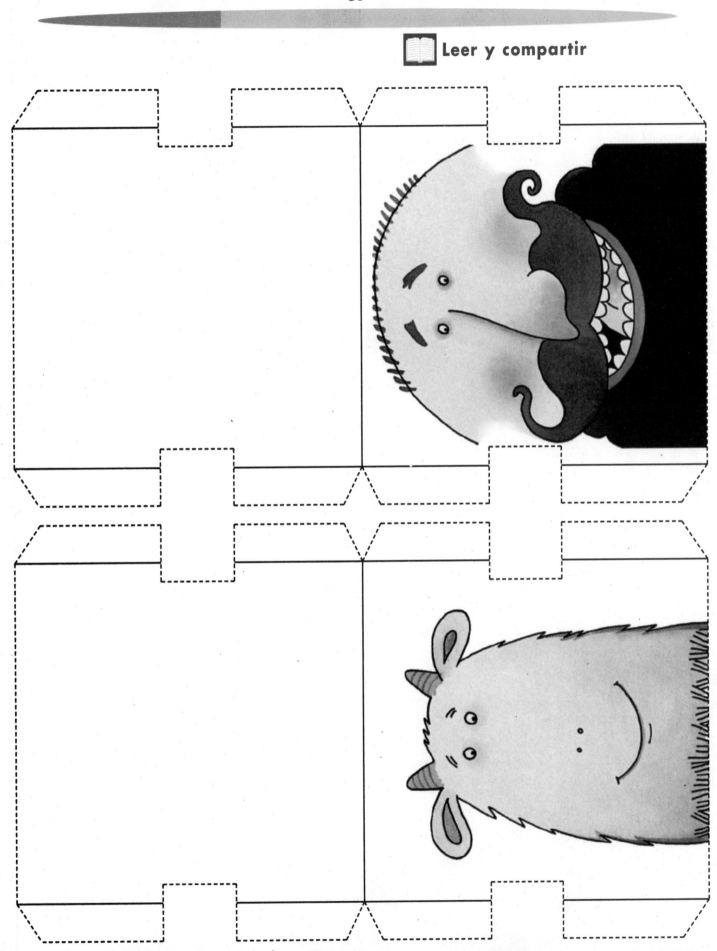

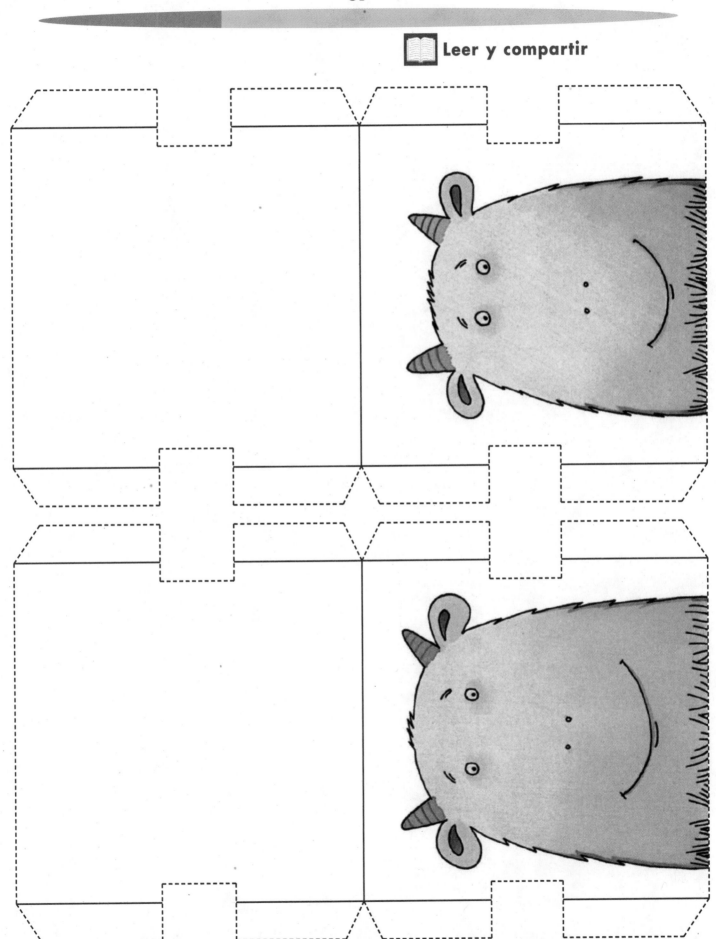

Tiempo de escribir

  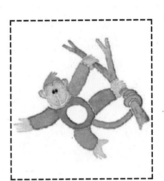

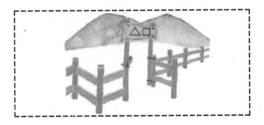

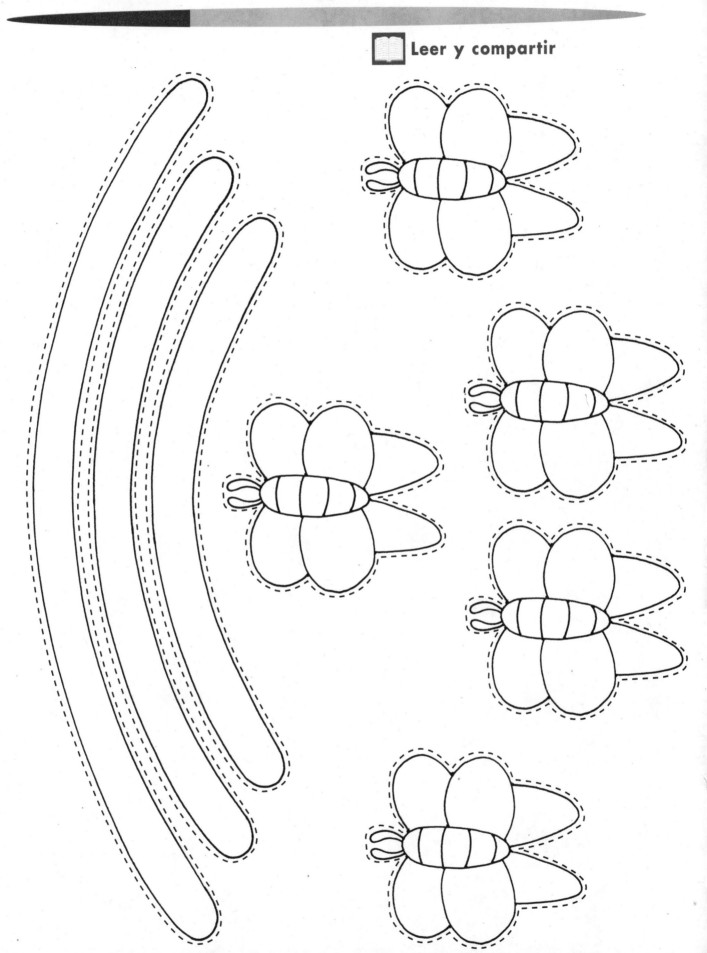

manubrio	pedales	asiento
llanta delantera	cadena	llanta trasera

25 • Los pececitos de colores

📖 **Leer y compartir**

Un día llegó un pececito de colores.

—¿Quién te dio esos colores?

El pececito Arco Iris dijo que era un secreto.

Si nos dices tu secreto, te haremos Rey.

📖 **Leer y compartir**

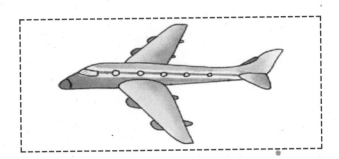

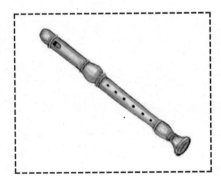

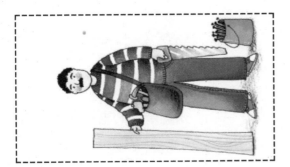

Tiempo de escribir

Fecha: ______________

Para: ______________________

____

____

De: ______________________

Fecha: ______________

Para: ______________________

____

____

De: ______________________

Tiempo de escribir

El gato escondió las ropas de Juan. El rey ordenó que le dieran al marqués uno de sus propios trajes.

El rey salió a pasear con su hermosa hija. El gato corrió hasta donde estaba Juan y le ordenó meterse al río.

Al morir, el padre de Juan le heredó un gato y unas botas. "¿Para qué quiero un gato?", pensaba Juan.

El gato llevó muchos regalos al rey y dijo que los enviaba su amo, el marqués de Carabás.

Al verlo tan elegante, la hija del rey se enamoró de Juan. Se casaron y vivieron muy felices.

El gato le dijo: —Si haces lo que yo te diga, serás feliz.

Hablar y escuchar

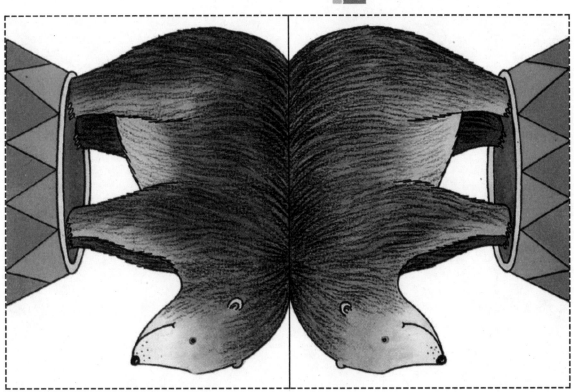

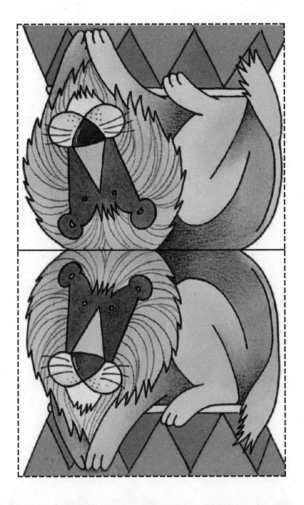

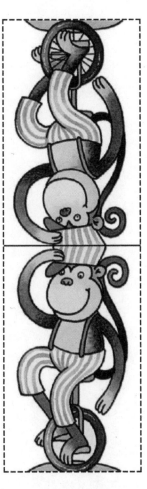

Hablar y escuchar

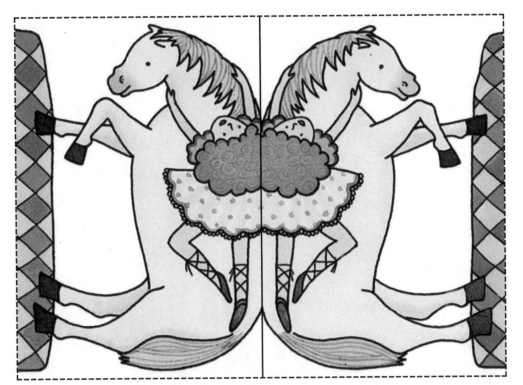

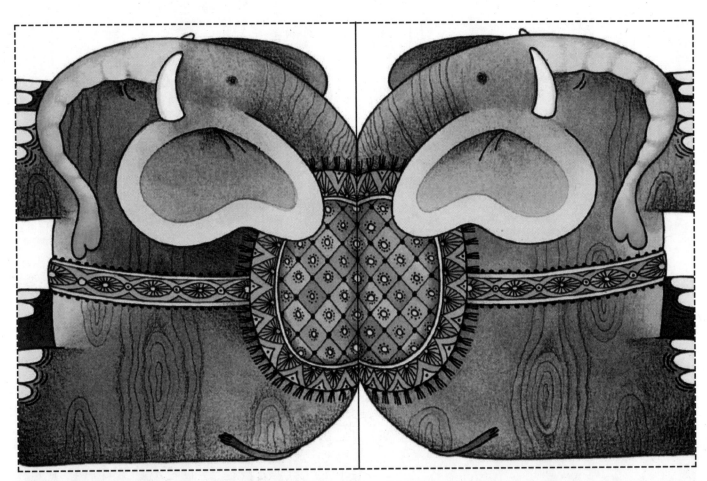

 **Leer y compartir**

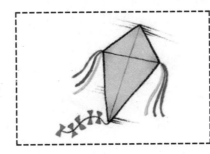

velero

helicóptero

dirigible

avioneta

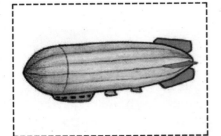

globo

avión

papalote

rehilete

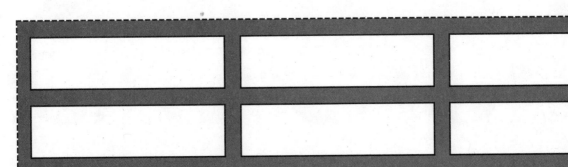

por eso me pongo traje de baño

por eso me pongo abrigo

por eso me pongo impermeable

y está nevando

y está lloviendo

y está granizando

Hace calor

Hace frío

Hace buen tiempo

Con el viento podemos
volar una cometa.

Al viento
no lo podemos ver.

El viento mueve las nubes
en el cielo.

La fuerza del viento
empuja la vela de un barco.

📖 **Leer y compartir**

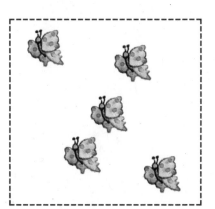

papagayo

palmera

huellas

barco

mariposas

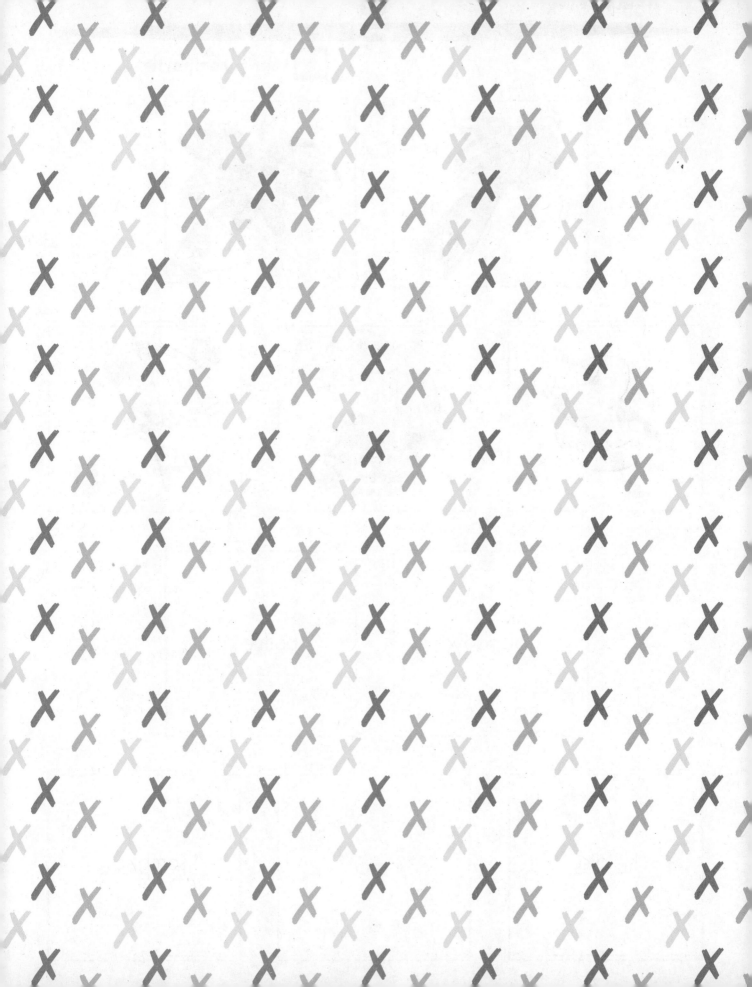

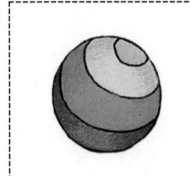

globos

payaso

pelota

elefante

sombrilla

📖 **Leer y compartir**

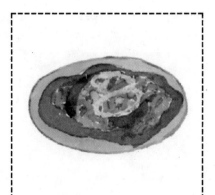

tortillas

chile

rallador

cuchillo

tostada

📖 **Leer y compartir**

huevo

gallina

pato

pollito

avestruz

carnicero

bombero

florero

gato

estambre

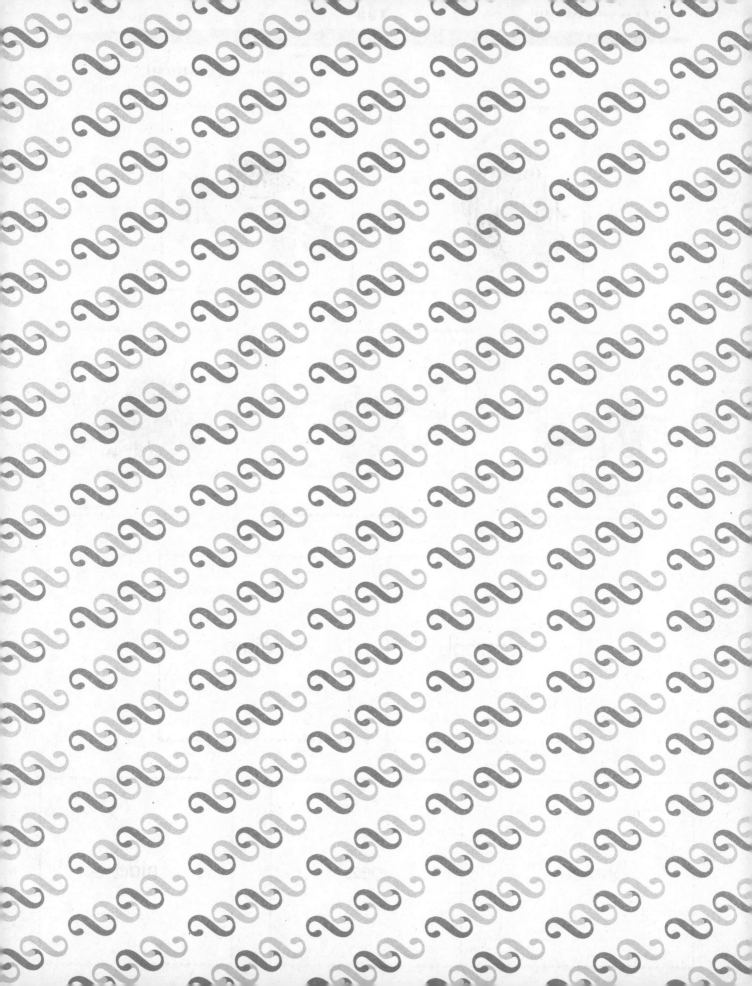

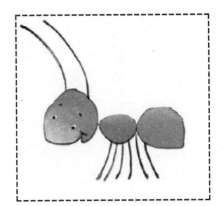

caracol

pájaro

hormiga

pez

nido

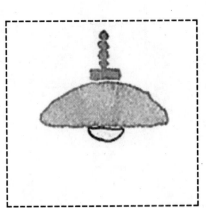

patines

tenis

botas

ratón

lámpara

sombrero

calcetines

zapatos

camisa

pantalón

Paco

vaca

casa

policía

perro

Haz dos sobres para las letras móviles.

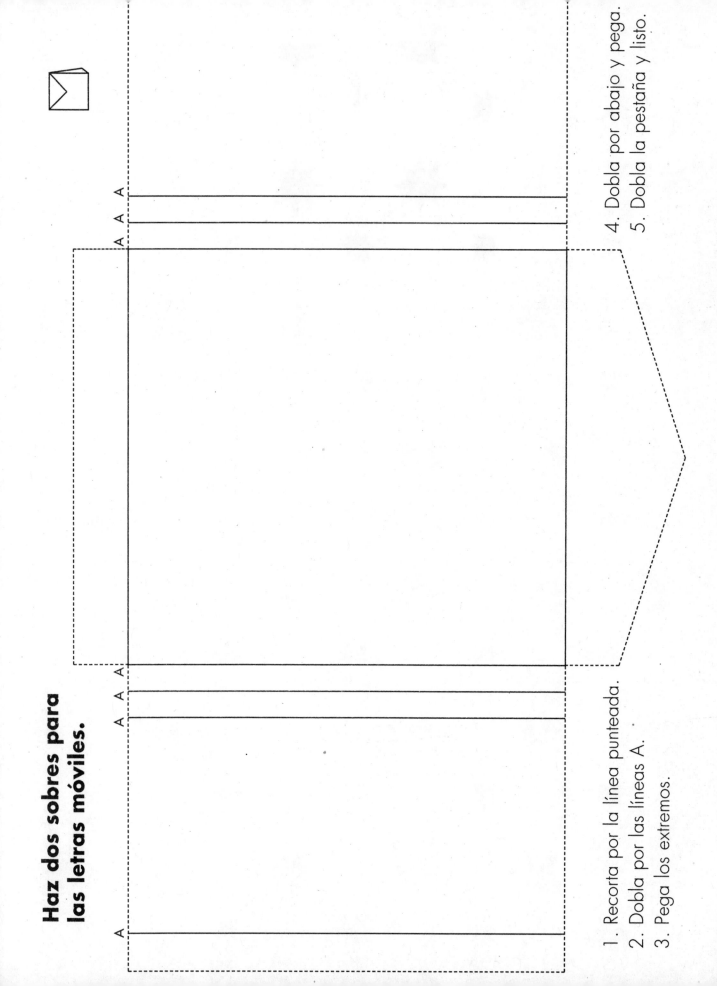

1. Recorta por la línea punteada.
2. Dobla por las líneas A.
3. Pega los extremos.
4. Dobla por abajo y pega.
5. Dobla la pestaña y listo.